THE MIRACLES OF JESUS:
What Really Happened?

Hubert J. Richards was born in 1921. He studied in Rome, where he took degrees in theology and in scripture. From 1949 to 1965 he taught scripture at St Edmund's College, Ware. From 1965 to 1972 he was principal of Corpus Christi College, the international institute of religious education in London. He is at present a lecturer in religious studies in the school of education of the University of East Anglia.

He is widely known, both in England and abroad, as a lecturer on the problems of religious education, and as a composer of a variety of gospel songs. He is author of *God Speaks To Us, Christ In Our World* (with Peter De Rosa), *What The Spirit Says To The Churches, An ABC Of The Bible, Forty Gospel Songs, Ten Gospel Songs, The Heart Of A Rose, Death And After: What Will Really Happen?, St Paul And His Epistles, What Happens When You Pray?, Pilgrim To The Holy Land, The Gospel In Song.*

By the same author in this series

The First Christmas: What Really Happened?
The First Easter: What Really Happened?

THE
MIRACLES OF JESUS:
What Really Happened?

AN INTRODUCTION TO
THE THEOLOGY OF JOHN

Hubert J. Richards

*Dedicated to the red rose,
my daily proof that
miracles are possible.*

MOWBRAY
LONDON & OXFORD

Acknowledgments

The author and publishers would like to acknowledge their indebtedness for permission to reproduce copyright material as follows: from *Miracles in Dispute* by E. and M.-L. Keller, published by SCM Press; 'In the Present Tense' by Sydney Carter from *The Two Way Clock*, © 1969 Stainer & Bell Ltd.

Scriptural quotations are taken from *The Jerusalem Bible* (copyright © 1966, 1967 and 1968 by Darton, Longman and Todd Ltd. and Doubleday and Company Inc. Used by permission of the publisher). The author has felt free to depart from this on a few occasions for the sake of precision.

Contents

1. Foreword   9

2. What Really Happened?   12

3. Water into Wine (John 2)   30

4. Life to the Dying (John 4–5)   39

5. Food in the Desert (John 6)   45

6. Walking on the Water (John 6)   60

7. Sight to the Blind (John 9)   67

8. New Life to the Dead (John 11)   82

9. Saved from Drowning (John 21)   95

10. Explaining the Miracles Away?   100

11. Postscript   114

    A Plan of John's Gospel   125

1. Foreword

A Ffolkes cartoon in *Punch* has two vaguely middle-eastern characters sitting disconsolately in a garden, with one sadly reminding the other: 'That was the year manna dropped from heaven. We just don't have summers like that any more.' No one can help feeling sympathy with the cartoon. Miracles belong to a bygone age. They just don't happen in the latterday, ordinary, humdrum world we live in.

In actual fact they do. A few years ago when I was in North America I saw a number of them take place before my very eyes. In the town where I was staying, Kathryn Kuhlman, an evangelist who has been on the road for twenty years, was holding a three-night stand before a packed auditorium of thousands. On each of the three nights she was able to convince a considerable number of her sick and crippled listeners that the Holy Spirit was there and then healing them, and dozens came up to the rostrum to bear witness to the fact that this was indeed so. Granted that some of her cures may have been planted *pour encourager les autres*, and that there was no indication of how long the electrifying effect of her preaching would last after she had left town, the spectacle was nonetheless awe-inspiring and moving.

But then 'miraculous' healings of this sort there have always been, in every country and century and culture, in religious contexts and outside them. A recent film featured the life story of another American evangelist, Marjoe Gortner (the unhappy forename derives from an over-enthusiastic combination of the words Mary and Joseph), who was groomed for an evangelistic career from the tender age of ten. Having had several hundred cures to his credit, he finally retired from the profession with the announcement that he had never believed in God, let alone in miracles, only in his excellent training as a persuasive preacher.

In County Cavan, Ireland, where seventh sons are regarded as endowed with powers denied to ordinary mortals, Finbar

Nolan, a seventh son 'squared' (his father was one too) is currently attracting enormous crowds who come to him to be healed of arthritis and ringworm. He does not call these cures miracles; he attributes his high rate of success quite simply to the confidence he and his patients have in his own healing powers.

In England, our own Harry Edwards has been conducting healing services in an explicitly religious context for over forty years. He attributes an alleged eighty per cent rate of success to the intervention of 'discarnate' doctors and healers who have passed over to the 'spirit world', and are wiser now than they once were on earth. He admits that the patient's belief in this other world, or indeed in God, is irrelevant to his cure.

Faith-healing of this kind has always been practised by religious and non-religious people alike, by rogues as well as by honest men. Those familiar with the healing stories of the New Testament will naturally want to ask where exactly the difference between the two lies. If these modern cures can be explained by 'natural' means, what is it about the cures attributed to Jesus which makes them supernatural? If faith-healing is so constant and recurrent a phenomenon in the history of man that it obviously proves very little, why do people assume that healings which take place in a Christian setting prove so much?

The proof-value of miracles, taken for granted in an earlier age, has been severely questioned by modern scholars. In fact the whole subject of the New Testament miracle stories, of their meaning and purpose, of their factual or symbolic basis, and of the extent to which this can be established by careful and unprejudiced scholarship – all this has been receiving considerable attention from theologians in recent years. Very little of their thought seems so far to have reached the general public, many of whom continue to read the gospel miracle stories with the naïveté with which they were once encouraged to read their Children's Bible Stories. They seem unaware that anyone has done any really sophisticated thinking on the subject. The result is that they either relegate miracles, like the two characters in the *Punch* cartoon, to a 'never-never' area of their lives or, being no longer able to accept unquestioningly such a literal understanding of the miracle stories, they imagine they have lost their faith.

The purpose of this book is to make the results of scholarship on this matter available to such people. Not that the experts are necessarily right. But those I have in mind remain dedicated Christians, and people have a right to know that it is possible to be a Christian without holding a nineteenth-century view of miracles.

Of course, some will say that such scholars have forfeited the right to call themselves Christians. But then they said the same a hundred years ago when scholars first suggested that a Christian need not hold a literalistic view of the six days of creation, or more recently when they suggested that it was possible to be a Christian and still be in favour of religious freedom, or ecumenism.

In this book, therefore, as in the others of this series,[1] my aim is not to propound any new or startling conclusions of my own, only to present as simply as I can what theologians are saying today on the subject of the miracles of Jesus. The sixteenth-century essayist Montaigne once concluded a lecture to a circle of French philosophers with words which I would like to make my own: 'Gentlemen, I have done nothing more than present you with flowers which others have picked. All I have contributed is the ribbon to tie them into a bouquet.'

[1] *The First Christmas: What Really Happened?*
The First Easter: What Really Happened?

2. What Really Happened?

A recent treatment of the gospel story of the feeding of the five thousand in the desert concludes with these words:

> It is *possible* to assume that there is some incident at the basis of the story, though its exact nature is difficult or impossible to determine now; but it can also be maintained that the story has been *generated* by the combination of two factors, the knowledge that Jesus as messiah was a prophet, the culmination of the line of previous prophets, and the memory that he worked wonders. Some generalised and summary accounts of cures are surely the product of this memory; they are founded on the general memory of his work rather than on that of any particular incident . . . It is perhaps not too much to suppose that, when this technique was applied to Jesus' role as the last and greatest of the line of prophets, quite a *trivial* incident may have been seen in this light as a sign, and described in a way which both brings out this aspect of Jesus and uses the knowledge that he did do such remarkable signs. (H. Wansbrough, *Event and Interpretation*, Sheed & Ward, London, 1973, pp. 79–80, my italics.)

Another author, dealing with the story of the stilling of the storm, has this comment to make:

> It is difficult to put one's finger on the fact which lies behind the story of the stilling of the storm, because even the traditional account of the event as it came to the Synoptics had already been given a theological meaning. Did the 'sign' consist of a miracle (in the ordinary sense of the word) in the cosmic order? Or is it rather a question of a series of [natural] circumstances in which the evangelists (and before

them Jesus himself) discerned the revelation of God? One would be tempted to think so, since Jesus explicitly refused to work wonders of a cosmic nature . . . It should be noted that in the similar story of the walking on the water . . . nothing more is said than that the storm stopped the moment Jesus got into the boat. (M.-E. Boismard, *Synopse des Quatre Evangiles*, Editions du Cerf, Paris, II, pp. 197–8.)

Both authors are Roman Catholics. Both are respected for the moderation and balance of their scholarship. Both, as the quotations show, are extremely cautious about the statements to which they are prepared to commit themselves. And yet, a critic might say, both seem strangely reluctant to allow a miracle to be a miracle. Why should this be so? Why this need to rationalize, to reduce, to water down? If the text suggests that something extraordinary took place, why not accept it at its face value? Why apparently try to turn it into something ordinary, even something 'quite trivial'?

There are several reasons for this cautious approach of scholars. They might best be discussed under the two headings of a new understanding of the world and of the gospels.

A NEW UNDERSTANDING OF THE WORLD

One of the characteristics of our century is its claim to have 'come of age'. The phrase is Dietrich Bonhoeffer's, and it is often quoted derisively. 'Look at the world we live in; has there ever been an age when men have been less mature and acted less like adults?' But Bonhoeffer never suggested that man had suddenly and miraculously become mature. He said that man has come of age, as an adolescent does at the age of eighteen, demanding the key of the door, and needing to be left free to solve life's problems on his own, without people giving him predetermined answers, least of all religious ones. He will not stomach them.

Where people of a previous age were content to live a life of unquestioning respect for authority, we ourselves live at a time

13

when authority of every kind is continually under scrutiny. The mood of modern man is to want to take charge of his own world, to shoulder what he sees as his own responsibilities instead of passing the buck to 'the authorities', whether these are civil or religious. Father-figures of all kinds are suspect, and this includes the Father-in-the-sky who featured so prominently in the traditional teaching of religion.

In other words, man today sees himself as left to his own devices, in a world which is autonomous. This means that he thinks of the universe he lives in as intelligible from within, on its own terms, with no need of something or someone 'outside' the universe to explain what makes it tick or to control it from a distance. In a pre-scientific age it was easy to speak of what could be explained as 'natural', and to attribute what could not be explained to the 'supernatural', whether this was thought of in terms of gods or demons, angels or fairies. But a scientific world can no longer function in this way. Not only has science inexorably narrowed the gaps in our knowledge, and therefore the scope of any possible 'supernatural' influence; it is confidently presumed that the remaining gaps also fall within the sphere of scientific explanation, and will eventually be filled as our knowledge of the world we live in progresses. It is interesting, for example, that the discussion a few years ago of Uri Geller's 'spoon bending' is carried on, even by those who take him seriously, not in supernatural but in natural terms of ESP, psychokinesis and parapsychology. It is taken for granted that there is a 'human' explanation, even if this has not yet fully come to light.

In a world such as this, there is less and less room – and ultimately there will be none – for the God of the gaps, the God who occasionally makes a miraculous intervention from outside.

The analysis given above is necessarily sketchy and generalized. It does not pretend to take into account the more recent phenomenon of a generation becoming rather disillusioned, and not a little frightened, by the totally secularized world it has inherited, and searching for a renewed sense of the transcendent in drugs, mysticism and the occult. But no one would question the fact that science has 'demythologized' some aspects of our world to an extent which makes the myth irretrievable as anything other than myth. Whether we like it or not, we are constitutionally unable to return to the mentality which saw lighning as a shaft of punishment expertly directed by God against the ungodly, and which spoke of the first lightning conductors, apparently deflecting the wrath of the heavens into the earth, as 'heretic rods'.

THE TEACHING OF JESUS

Now, however irreligious this modern world-view may sound, it strangely echoes the teaching of Jesus. A father does not feel threatened when he sees his child grow into a man: he is delighted. A father attending his son's coming-of-age party does not begrudge him the independence he will now wield, or weep over his own diminishing authority: he says, with great pride, 'That's my boy.' And God is like that, Jesus said, he himself being a living illustration of that fact, the manly Son of God with a supreme sense of freedom which he wanted all God's children to share.

This message of his emerges particularly clearly in what he says about the Kingdom of God, a topic which Matthew, Mark and Luke place at the centre of his teaching.

The later pages of the Old Testament refer frequently to the Kingdom or Rule of God. The naïve hope that it could be identified with the kingdom of Israel had by that time been abandoned, and the dispirited conviction was growing that it could only be brought about by a direct intervention of God. As this intervention failed to materialize, the Kingdom was gradually relegated to the more and more distant future, to the 'age to come'.

Jesus' preaching seems to have been specifically directed against this rather pessimistic (and it should be added, undemanding) view of the Kingdom of God. In story after story he insists that the Kingdom of God is not like that, because God is not like that. The Kingdom is not some miraculous panacea which an absentee God in his distant heaven will in his own good time intervene to bring about. It is not in such a heaven or in the future at all. It is here on earth, in the present, now, within man's grasp; indeed it always has been. It is not out there, but down here.

> He made his way through towns and villages preaching, and proclaiming the *Good* News of the Kingdom of God (Luke 8:1).
> I have *seen* the 'end of all things' already take place – Satan falling like lightning from heaven (Luke 10:18).
> The Kingdom of God *has* already overtaken you (Luke 11:20).
> The Kingdom of God is *here* in your midst, among you (Luke 17:21).

This, ultimately, was the 'heresy' of Jesus, the issue which finally pushed people to kill him: he was taking away their comfortable and undemanding ideas of God, and asking them to focus their attention on man. Certainly the charge levelled against the first Christians was that they were atheists. They had secularized everything and depopulated the heavens, which for 'religious' people was intolerable. They were saying what Jesus had said before them, that there was no God out there who would finally and miraculously usher in Kingdom Come. It was up to men to bring it about, and the only time they had was the present. When men realized this, and in their anguish cried out, 'God, where on earth are you?' they would hear God's reply, 'On earth, in your midst. I'm not outside your work, as you thought. I'm in it.'

God was no longer to be thought of as living and acting in a sacred area of his own. He was active in man, and could be discovered only in the most 'secular' of all realities, man's daily life.

MIRACLES IN A SECULAR WORLD

It is this understanding of the secular as the place in which God reveals himself that has set scholars searching for a more

16

human explanation of the miracle stories in the bible. They are asking whether we should not be trying to understand them as part of the reality we know, and not somehow outside it. They are asking whether the extraordinary aspect of the stories has not misled us and sent us looking up to heaven, whereas they ought to be explicable in more 'earthy' terms.

In his study of the often misleading distinction we make between the 'natural' and the 'supernatural', the Jesuit Fr Schoonenberg suggests that it is quite possible for God to use creaturely causes for things that appear to us as miracles. In fact, one would expect him to do so, because God's way of acting vis-à-vis his creatures is not the same as the way creatures act upon each other. With two creatures, what one does the other cannot do. But the case is not the same with creator and creature. If it were, the creator would be in competition with his creature, and reduced to the status of creature. In the case of creator and creature, 'What God does the creature also does; what God does not do neither does the creature; that which God does more the creature also does more; that which God does less the creature also does less.' They are never rivals.

God's power is not diminished when he uses creatures as causes in the ordinary course of events; his power at the heart of every rose is no less real for being 'natural'. Why then should the same not be true in 'miraculous' events, even if the created cause is more difficult for us to perceive? And if this is so, we need not think of miracles as 'interventions' of God or interferences with the ordinary course of nature. Nor is there any reason to exclude them from our secular understanding of the world. (See P. Schoonberg, *Covenant and Creation*, Sheed & Ward, London, 1968, pp. 170 ff.)

MIRACLES AND FAITH

Some may feel that this approach to miracles leaves precious little room for the exercise of faith. If everything is to be explained in human, this-world terms, what happens to faith?

17

Is not faith precisely a refusal to be limited by human reason and worldly wisdom, a willingness to abandon onself to God beyond the limits of what the eye can see and the mind measure? If a Christian insists on making his own reason the measure of everything, how is he distinguishable from the rationalist and humanist? Is he not contradicting St Paul who, with his healthy mistrust of 'the wisdom of the wise and the learning of the learned', says that faith must be an obstacle and an offence to human intellectualism and self-sufficiency? Is he not doing precisely what Paul refused to do, namely tailoring his faith to the requirements of unbelieving man?

It is interesting that there is not a word in Paul's epistles about Jesus' miracles. In fact, in the passage I have just alluded to, he even states that while miracles would provide very acceptable 'motives of credibility' for certain people, they do not constitute the challenge that Christian faith offers to human reason:

> While the Jews demand miracles
> and the Greeks look for wisdom,
> here are we preaching a crucified Christ;
> to the Jews an obstacle that they cannot get over,
> to the pagans madness (1 Corinthians 1:22–3).

Clearly what Paul sees as the well-night insurmountable obstacle which Christianity presents to the intellectual is not its 'miraculous' aspect, but the cross. The object of faith is not a number of mind-boggling prodigies which the Christian is asked to accept *quia absurdum*, but the foolishness of the cross, the scandalous reversal of values represented by the claim that God is revealed and the world saved in the shameful death of one rejected by political and religious authorities alike.

Christian faith therefore does not mean that reason should be abandoned, but that it should be correctly orientated. And the offence with which reason is confronted is not an intellectual hindrance . . . like some of the miracles; it is the difficulty of believing, practically and existentially, that love

18

overcomes death. (E. and M.-L. Keller, *Miracles in Dispute*, SCM, London, 1969, p. 190.)

This refusal to depreciate the human reason, or to diminish a sense of individual responsibility, is in line with Jesus' own preaching. It emerges clearly from the reply he is reported to have made on the occasion of the cleansing of the temple, when he was asked, 'What authority have you for acting like this?' (Matthew 21:23). His contemporaries were expecting him to produce visible and tangible credentials for his way of acting. The fourth gospel even mentions a request for a 'sign' or miracle to back up this extraordinary exercise of personal authority (John 2:18). Jesus refuses to comply, and simply throws the question back, 'John's baptism, where did it come from, heaven or man?' and there the discussion ends. He was asking people to make a personal decision, first about John and then about himself. They had heard both John and Jesus preaching, and had to make up their own minds about whether or not the preaching was from God. Any external 'proof', miraculous or otherwise, would only confuse the issue. Truth is its own witness, and external authority can only point towards it, not legitimate it.

If one describes Jesus' views, as reflected in his rejection of the demand for signs, from the point of view of the history of thought, it may be said that his proclamation liberated man's personal power of judgment by appealing to his personal conviction and individual conscience. In this way Jesus declared man to be of age, autonomous. Traditional belief in the truth of the written law . . . was, like faith on the basis of external signs and miracles, an externally motivated and heteronomous faith; people believed because it was written in the Scriptures, because it was asserted by other people who ought to know. The faith in God which Jesus preached springs from the inner conviction and recognition that God is right . . . Because it encouraged an independent judgment towards the official interpretation of the law, the proclamation of Jesus meant that the individual was set free to criticize the institution. It was this which made Jesus' preaching seem dangerous to authoritative Jewish quarters. (E. and M.-L. Keller, *op. cit.* pp. 231–2.)

It was this kind of human independence and confident maturity that Jesus recommended to his disciples, with the warning that they could expect the same fate as his. He launched them on their mission, in loneliness, but with the assurance that nothing was impossible. They would work even greater miracles than he had worked, through their deep faith that God can do wonders. But not mere physical miracles; they would be responsible for bringing about the very Kingdom of God, the transformation of the world. Their faith would be their conviction that God was strong enough to overcome evil in the historical and secular world in which they lived. Their faith would be that God is present here and now, working *in* history and not outside it, first in Jesus of Nazareth, and then in all those who are inspired by his Spirit.

THE RELUCTANT WONDER WORKER

This emphasis on the secular in the teachings of both Paul and Jesus is corroborated by a whole series of gospel texts which, far from stressing the miraculous element in Jesus' ministry, strangely play it down.

For the purposes of apologetical argument, we tend to present the gospel as a series of miracle stories to which Jesus kept pointing as proof that he was sent by God and that his message was true. We conveniently neglect an equally strong gospel tradition that he was frequently embarrassed by the wonders that accompanies his mission. He seems to have had considerable reservations about what they might or might not prove. 'Divine interventions' are precisely what he refused to associate himself with.

This tradition appears on the very first page of the gospels, where Jesus is shown as turning down the temptation to play the popular role of a wonder working messiah, one who would solve all problems by floating down from the heavens or turning stones into bread (Matthew 4:1 ff). This story is deliberately placed at the beginning of the account of Jesus' ministry, where it stands as a parable of a whole life-time of resistance to such a temptation. It is echoed again in the story of Peter's suggestion that Jesus should avoid the deadly conflict awaiting him in Jerusalem, a suggestion which is repudiated with some vehemence with the words, 'Get behind me, Satan!' (Matthew 16:23). It appears for a last time in the Gethsemane story where Jesus is shown hoping and even praying for a miraculous escape from the fate that lies ahead of him, and finally accepting it as the will of God (Matthew 26:36ff.).

When the court official at Capernaum asks Jesus to come and cure his son who is at the point of death, his reported reply is, 'So you will not believe unless you see signs and portents!' – and it is meant as a rebuke (John 4:48). So is his comment to the crowds who are following him after being fed in the desert: 'I tell you most solemnly, you are not looking for me because you have seen (understood) the signs, but because you had all the food you wanted to eat!' (John 6:26).

In fact the working of miracles, far from proving someone to be of God, could prove the very opposite. Many of those who eventually claim to have cast out demons and worked miracles in the name of Jesus will be told to their faces, 'I have never known you; away from me, you evil men!' (Matthew 7:23). Signs and portents, even such as could lead the elect astray, are the signature tune by which one can recognize a *false* Christ (Matthew 24:24), in much the same way as a false prophet is to be recognized according to the Deuteronomic Code:

> If a prophet . . . arises among you and offers to do a sign or a wonder for you, even if the sign or wonder comes about, if he then says to you, 'Come, then let us follow other gods' . . . you are not to listen to the words of that prophet . . . That prophet . . . must be put to death for he has preached apostasy (Deuteronomy 13:2–6).

In short, the demand for miracles as proofs, as Paul was later to point out, is the mark of an unbeliever, of an enemy of Christ rather than of a disciple. When the Pharisees and Sadducees asked him to produce a sign from heaven to authenticate his preaching, he declined, and called them an evil and faithless generation for making such a demand (Matthew 16:1–4). When Herod's playboy son Antipas hoped that his dull afternoon would be enlivened by a miracle performed by the Galilean prisoner paraded before him, Jesus refused to humour his whim (Luke 23:8). And when those who put Jesus to death mocked him by offering to believe if he stepped down from his cross, they discovered that this is precisely what the true messiah will not do, because he cannot (Matthew 27:40·2).

The gospel tradition of Jesus as a reluctant wonder worker is a strong one. It should not be neglected, as it often has been, in a discussion of the New Testament miracles.

TAKING THE INCARNATION SERIOUSLY

Perhaps many of our difficulties over the miracle stories of the gospels stem from the fact that we do not, on the whole, take the incarnation very seriously. We say we believe in a God who became man and showed himself to be at one with us in our earthly situation. But we go on acting as if God were separated from the world and man, distant and remote. The word 'nature' denotes for us either a closed reality which cannot suffer any intrusion at all (the viewpoint of the materialist), or a reality which is usually closed but which permits an occasional intrusion from the 'supernatural' (the viewpoint of those who think of God as 'intervening').

Is not Christianity the good news that we need not hold either of these dismal world pictures? That reality is indeed one, single and homogeneous, without anything existing 'outside' of it. But the heavenly is not thereby shut out. It is from now on, for ever, to be found *in* the earthly, and only there. Jesus has demythologized the 'supernatural'.

Where does the peculiarity and uniqueness of the Christian

22

message lie? Certainly not in the fact that in the stories of the bible supernatural forces intervene in the historical world – phenomena of this kind may be found in all the ancient religions – but in the way in which God and heaven are designated, in concrete terms, here on earth. The origin of this concrete designation, the source of 'revelation' in Christianity is, however, a particular earthly person. 'He who has seen me has seen the Father.' (E. and M.-L. Keller, *op. cit*. p. 209. The preceding paragraphs owe much to this excellent book, as anyone who has read it will recognize.)

To sum up, then, what has been said so far. When today's students of the gospel miracles are asked what really happened, one of the reasons why they are reluctant to give as simple and uncritical a reply as was once customary is that they share a new understanding of the world they live in. It is a thoroughly secular world, intelligible in its own terms, with no gaps which need to be plugged by the 'supernatural'. They expect, therefore, to be able to understand what really happened in natural terms, without resorting to explanations that go beyond nature. Nor does such a world-view undermine the teaching of Jesus. In fact it coincides squarely with his insistence that the Kingdom of God is not to be looked for in the heavens, but here on earth among men. It is in human terms that God has revealed himself, not in extra-human ones.

A NEW UNDERSTANDING OF THE GOSPELS

But that is not the only reason why scholars of our day have taken a new approach to the miracles. They have also arrived at a completely new understanding of the documents from which we derive our knowledge of Jesus' miracles – the gospels. These documents, which at first sight look like nothing more than biographies of an earthly Jesus have, after a century of critical analysis, been shown to be something far more valuable, a proclamation of the risen Christ.

Christians are usually not sufficiently aware of how central and foundational to their faith is the death and resurrection of Jesus. When they have spoken of this, they have already expressed what their faith is about. When they have not, they have not yet begun to speak about Christianity. Any 'doctrine' in their mind which they cannot relate to the death and resurrection of Jesus is not part of the Christian faith.

In other words, when a Christian is asked, 'What do you believe in? What makes sense of your life?' his reply cannot simply be, 'God'; even the non-Christian can and must say that. He has to reply, 'The God who is the Father of our Lord Jesus Christ.' And when he is pressed, 'Where do you know what that God is like?' he has to reply, 'In the death and resurrection of Jesus Christ.'

This is really the only thing that the gospels are about. I do not mean that they all come to a climax with the death and resurrection of Jesus – that is obvious enough. I mean that they all *begin* with his death and resurrection. And this not only in the sense that none of the gospels were written until after the resurrection had taken place – that too is obvious. But the gospels were deliberately composed to make the risen Christ present to the reader through the ages.

A gospel is not a biography of someone who lived in the past. It is a proclamation of faith in someone who lives on today. That is its 'literary form', and if this does not influence the way we read the gospel we will misunderstand it. That goes above all for the miracle stories. They must not be read as simple biography and mistaken for chronicles of marvels which took place a long time ago. They are first of all a proclamation of what the risen Christ means for the writer, and they are issued as an invitation to the reader to discover the same reality in his own life. The reader of the miracle stories must ask himself, 'Is the risen Christ the food without which I will die in the desert, the one who can transform my life like water into wine? Is Christ for me the one who can walk on the waters of death and enable me to share this power? Is Christ the healer of the deformities in my life, the creator in me of a life which is more fully human?

If a gospel is a piece of literature of that kind, then we can no longer put directly to any of its stories the merely biographical question, 'What really happened?' If the author did not pretend to produce a biography but a profession of his faith, then the only question we are entitled to put is, 'What does this story mean to someone who has seen the risen Lord?' as had the community which first told the story, as had the evangelist who used that story for his own purpose, and as has the reader to whom the gospel is addressed. The biographical question is a secondary one, which it may in some cases be possible to answer though there can be no guarantee of this, given the type of literature that a gospel is. The primary question it is always possible to answer. And if the gospels hold light of that kind for us, it is rather pointless to keep on asking if they hold water.

We tend to be shy, if not terrified, of approaching the miracle stories in this way. Whatever the scholars may do with the rest of the New Testament, we think, do not for God's sake let them touch these, otherwise we shall have nothing left. These are the 'proof texts', and if they don't leave these intact, we will no longer know where we are.

If that expresses our own concern, then for us miracles have remained at the level of the famous story of the golf match between St Peter and St Paul, where the first three holes are played in utter silence, each successfully holing in one, and as Peter is sizing up his shot for the fourth the silence is broken by Paul who says, 'All right, let's cut out the miracles and play a round of golf.'

In that context, a miracle is simply the impossible, the inexplicable, the obviously and inescapably supernatural. In that context, the apostles would have had to say to Jesus – as we imagine ourselves saying, 'Unless you do something sensational, I shall not believe. First of all do something that I can't explain and can't get out of, and force me to accept you, otherwise I won't.'

Very little reflection is needed to realize how idiotic this would be. To begin with, a 'faith' which was forced on anyone like that, simply because he could find no other way out, would not be faith. Certainly Jesus repudiates it on page after page of the gospel, as we saw above. Again and again he demands faith *before* the cure that is to take place, not after. In Nazareth he is reported to be unable to work miracles precisely because the preliminary faith and goodwill is lacking (Matthew 13:58). Whatever he could have done among his compatriots, it would not have proved anything or indeed made any sense.

Moreover, at this level of inexplicable wonders, the miracles of Jesus were presumably seen by everyone in his audience, including his enemies. The gospel narrative states on many occasions that this was so. Yet they did not feel forced to conclude that Jesus was the Son of God.

But then neither did his own disciples. Whatever it was that they saw in Jesus' lifetime, it all went for nothing at Calvary. Here was someone who gave every promise of being the long-awaited messianic liberator of his people, but as far as they were concerned it was now quite clear that he was not. 'Our own hope had been that he would be the one to set Israel free,' but he is dead, and therefore obviously won't be (Luke 23:21).

It is not until after their resurrection experience – whatever it is that this consisted of and however it is to be explained – that the disciples were convinced that Jesus is the Son of God. That was the turning point, the crucial moment. That was the event in the story of Jesus which revolutionized everything they had so far experienced him to be. In the light of that one event, all the rest could be no more than an anticlimax, stories of miracles included. Turn water into wine? But that's nothing! The person I know can turn hell into heaven.

The Christian therefore cannot say to Jesus, just as the first disciples could not say, 'First prove yourself, and then I will see if I can commit myself to you.' What comes first is the resurrection of Jesus and our experience of it, which is itself a commitment to him. It is because we have committed ourselves first, and in that commitment discovered who he is, that we can go on to read and accept the stories in which he stills storms and walks on water, multiplies loaves and raises

the dead. None of these stories can ever do more than evoke the
one wonder of his resurrection.

TAKING THE MIRACLES SERIOUSLY

My aim in this book is to take the miracle stories seriously, as
illustrations of what Christ means to one who has seen him as
his risen Lord. It seems to me that the many attempts to
'biographize' the miracle stories do not take them seriously
enough. To spend countless pages discussing the historical
nature of the event on which a story is based, and to end with a
footnote on the theological meaning of the event in the eyes of
the evangelist – this is to trivialize the story. It is certainly to
do the very opposite of what the evangelist did; he was usually
so intent on the theological meaning of the story that he had no
time to consider its historical reality.

This is especially true of John, who calls all his miracles
'signs'. They point to something beyond themselves. They
indicate the kind of reality brought about not simply by some
prodigious event of the past but by the person of Jesus himself.
It is Jesus, in his own person, who brings sight to the blind,
who feeds the hungry and who gives life.

This book concentrates on the 'significant' miracles presented in John's gospels. If these stories had been read in the pages
of Matthew, Mark or Luke, one might be forgiven for
mistaking them for simple pieces of reporting. In John this is
impossible. He fills the stories with so much symbolism, and
surrounds them with so much theological discourse, that it is
obvious he is dealing with something more than strange
happenings: these are signs of a more profound reality.

John uses symbolism in a way which turns upside down the
accepted meanings of the words 'real' and 'symbolic'. In
normal speech, the historical event would be regarded as the
real thing, and the theological interpretation of it as 'only
symbolic'. For John, the real thing is always the risen
Christ – it is he who is the *true* Bread, Wine, Water, Shepherd.
The symbol is everything else – bread, wine, water and
shepherds, whether they are miraculous or not. These have far

27

less reality than the central fact, which is the death and resurrection of Jesus.

This is not to prejudge the factual basis of the stories contained in John's gospel, or to suggest that he is not interested in history. Given his central thesis that, in Jesus, God's Word became flesh, he is clearly very interested indeed, and a de-historicized Jesus would be of no use to his theology. Anyone who examines the pages of this gospel will see that they are punctuated with historical and geographical details, as if to emphasize that the theology of these pages is really en-fleshed.

The messianic demonstration in Jerusalem, for instance, takes place in the forty-sixth year of the Jerusalem temple rebuilding programme (John 2:20). The disciples whom Jesus invites to follow him are called – it is almost as if they were looking at their watches – at 4.00 pm (1:39). Jesus arrives at the well of Samaria and sits down there at midday precisely (4:6). The unusual depth of the well is remarked on (4:11), and anyone who has visited it will understand why. The word used for the well is not the normal one, *phrear*, but *pēgē*, which means 'spring', and this is what the well is, being fed by an underground stream (4:6, 14). The pool of Bethzatha is described as being spanned by five arches (5:2), and though this suggests an improbable shape, the detail was corroborated in 1871 by archaeologists who revealed four sides of a rectangle intersected by an arch across the middle. Examples could be multiplied. The point very simply is that the reader of John's gospel cannot ask, 'Does he want to present theology or narrate events?' For John, the events *are* theology, and history *is* the mystery of God revealing himself. The Word of God has truly become flesh.

What needs to be added, however, in the words of John himself, is that the flesh of itself avails nothing; it is only the Spirit that can give life (John 6:63). If through this flesh we cannot see the Spirit, we are wasting our time.

This book is concerned, as the evangelist was concerned, to find the Spirit behind the miracle stories, and to discover them as 'deep stories rather than tall stories', as Professor Barclay calls them. I wish to read them, as the evangelist told them, with hindsight and in retrospect. I wish deliberately to ask rather few questions about their historical reality, because these questions are frequently impossible to answer. I wish rather to make a meditation on the miracle stories. I wish to ask, with the evangelist, 'What do these stories mean for someone who has seen the risen Christ?' as he had, and as I have. How else could I call myself a Christian?[1]

[1] A plan of John's gospel will be found on p. 125.

3. Water into Wine

(John 2)

On the third day there was a wedding at Cana in Galilee. The mother of Jesus was there, and Jesus and his disciples had also been invited. When they ran out of wine, since the wine provided for the wedding was all finished, the mother of Jesus said to him, 'They have no wine'. Jesus said, 'Woman, why turn to me? My hour has not come yet.' His mother said to the servants, 'Do whatever he tells you'. There were six stone water jars standing there, meant for the ablutions that are customary among the Jews; each could hold twenty or thirty gallons. Jesus said to the servants, 'Fill the jars with water', and they filled them to the brim. 'Draw some out now' he told them 'and take it to the steward.' They did this; the steward tasted the water, and it had turned into wine. Having no idea where it came from – only the servants who had drawn the water knew – the steward called the bridegroom and said, 'People generally serve the best wine first, and keep the cheaper sort until the guests have had plenty to drink; but you have kept the best wine till now'.

This was the first of the signs given by Jesus: it was given at Cana in Galilee. He let his Glory be seen, and his disciples believed in him (John 2:1–11).

LOOKING FOR CLUES

To discover the theological meaning which lies behind the stories narrated by John, it is important to look for the clues which he has placed there. The present passage offers several.

To begin with the closing phrase: the event is spoken of as the first of the signs offered by Jesus to point to his true identity. It can be disputed whether it was historically the first or not, since the very next sign, the cleansing of the temple, is placed at the end of Jesus' ministry by Matthew, Mark and Luke. All the same it is clear that John wants it first. For him this is a very significant story, summing up the meaning of all that is to follow. He wants it on page one, in much the same way that Matthew, Mark and Luke insist on putting Jesus' baptism and temptation on their opening page. The story of Jesus' baptism and temptation forms a kind of précis of his life, a preview of his death and resurrection. So does this story of the wedding at which water became wine.

The story therefore begins 'on the third day'. It is strange that the English version of the Jerusalem Bible should have translated this phrase as 'three days later'. True, a footnote relates the Cana event to the sequence of events in the preceding chapter, and the translator is allowed to draw attention to the fact that this was apparently intended by the author. But not to the extent of obliterating his original phrase, which the French *Bible de Jérusalem* has been careful to preserve. If this gospel was written towards the end of the first century, when the phrase 'the third day' had already become a familiar part of the Christian creed about the resurrection (the three gospel predictions of the passion suggest that this was so, as do the credal formulas in Acts 10:40 and 1 Corinthians 15:4), then it is unthinkable that it would not have those overtones when used here.

Any doubts on that score would be dispelled by the further clue contained in the word 'Glory', which this event or sign is said to manifest. In biblical terms the word 'glory' has a far stronger sense than it has acquired in our usage. For us, someone's glory is his reputation or renown, something external to him; it tells us little, if anything, of his inner worth. For the biblical writers, the inner worth is precisely what the 'glory' of a person is. And when the word is applied to God, the 'Glory' is a synonym for God himself. It means the very reality of God insofar as it is manifested to men.

Now John uses the word 'Glory' of Jesus' crucifixion and resurrection. It occurs with special frequency in the farewell discourses, where Jesus refers again and again to the 'Glory' to which he is about to go. 'What God is' will be most clearly manifested in Jesus' death and resurrection. And this is simply taking up a theme which is present throughout this gospel. On its opening page it announces that the Word which was with

31

God became flesh so that men could clearly see the Glory (John 1:14). Later it forewarns us that we cannot see it fully until Jesus has himself been glorified on the cross (7:39). The passion story finally begins with the words: 'Now the Hour has come for the Son of man to be glorified' (12:23). Clearly, when John says that 'Jesus manifested his Glory', he is saying something about his death and resurrection.

So the word 'Hour' provides another clue. Those not on the watch for clues might imagine that when Jesus says, 'My Hour has not come yet', he means something like, 'The time for doing miracles has not yet started', or even – as I have seen one commentator naïvely suggest – 'Yes all right, Mother, I'll do it in a moment.' A closer look at John's gospel would have revealed that the word 'Hour' is used throughout in a technical sense. Jesus' public ministry is twice punctuated with the note that his enemies were unable to arrest him 'because his Hour had not yet come' (John 7:30, 8:20), and the account of his passion begins with the rubric, 'Now the Hour has come' (12:23). The thought of it fills him with anguish, and he prays to be saved from this Hour (12:27). The final passover meal is introduced with the title, 'Jesus knew that the Hour had come for him to pass over from this world' (13:1), and ends with the prayer, 'Father, the Hour has come: glorify your Son' (17:1). In short, the word 'Hour' in the Cana story is yet another reference to Jesus' coming death and resurrection.

A further clue is to be found in the mention of Jesus' mother, since the only other mention of her in this gospel is on the last page, where John is meditating on the meaning of the scene at Calvary. Given the frequency with which John uses the literary device known as *inclusio* – whereby the end of a section recalls a detail mentioned at the beginning to allow the two ends to be tied together – it would be very surprising if this cross-reference was not intentional here. That it is quite deliberate is further suggested by the unusual title given in both places to Jesus' mother: 'Woman, why turn to me?' (2:4); 'Woman, this is your son' (19:26). Now it is quite possible that this was a perfectly respectful form of address, not a snub but the equivalent of 'Madam' or 'Lady'. Even so it is odd. One would expect Jesus to say 'Mother' not 'Madam'. Why the word 'Woman'? In the context of the Calvary scene it falls easily into place. There John is recalling text after text (the margin of the Jerusalem Bible notes four explicit quotations and numerous allusions) to point to Jesus as the climax of Old Testament hopes. And among these Mary is presented as the counterpart of the Woman who stands at the head of the Old Testament, the 'Mother of all those who have life' (Genesis 3:20). At Calvary, Mary is the Mother of all who have life to the full – those 'whom Jesus loves' (John 19:26). And Cana is meant to be a preview of this truth.

These clues, and the areas into which they lead us, should warn us in advance of the inappropriateness of some of the questions which commentators love to ask, and even try to answer! Questions such as 'How far is it from Nazareth to Cana?' 'Who was invited to the wedding?' 'Was Jesus related to the bridegroom?' 'How many gallons are there in a Hebrew or Greek "measure"?' do not begin to touch John's thoughts, let alone fathom them.

THE WEDDING BANQUET

But lest we miss the wood for the trees, let us look at the principal clue this passage offers us to John's thinking. He puts what he wants to say in the setting of a wedding. The setting would be familiar to anyone who had read the other three gospels, where Jesus' mission and work is often described in terms of a marriage. In Matthew 9:15 Jesus defends the lack of asceticism in the life of his disciples with the words: 'Surely the bridegroom's attendants would never think of mourning as long as the bridegroom is still with them. But the time will come for the bridegroom to be taken away, and then they will fast.' In Matthew 22:1 and 11 he tells two parables in which the Kingdom of God is compared to a prince's wedding feast to which everyone is invited. And Matthew 25 repeats the figure of speech to compare the Kingdom to the situation where ten bridesmaids set out in procession to meet the bridegroom.

When Luke picks up the theme, he has Jesus talking of the

need to pick a seat near the bottom of the wedding table, since only the man who humbles himself in this way will be exalted (Luke 14:11). And when he comes back to the theme again Jesus asks, 'Who is the greater: the one at table or the one who serves? Yet here am I among you as one who serves' (Luke 22:27). The implication is that the one who provides the meal is brought lowest – as he himself will be in death – before he is exalted.

The theme of humiliation and exaltation is a refinement, though we shall see its application in a moment. But the more general theme of the gospel pages, where the future Kingdom of God is compared to the joy of a wedding, and of a wedding banquet – that was a commonplace among the Old Testament prophets. It is taken up for a last time in the closing pages of the New Testament:

> And I seemed to hear the voices of a huge crowd, like the sound of the ocean or the great roar of thunder, answering, 'Alleluia! The Kingdom of the Lord our God Almighty has begun; let us be glad and joyful and give praise to God, because this is the time for the marriage of the Lamb. His bride is ready . . . Happy are those who are invited to the wedding feast of the Lamb' (Revelation 19:6–9).

THE JOYS OF WINE

The wine at the wedding feast is part of that general theme. Of itself, wine is a natural enough symbol of joy, as was appreciated even by that ascetical saint Thomas Aquinas, who went on record with the opinion that 'if a man deliberately abstains from wine to such an extent that he does serious harm to his nature, he will not be free from blame' (*Summa Theologiae* 2a2ae, 150, 1). But in the context of Kingdom Come, wine is a symbol of the longed-for joys of the future age, and occurs as such in many of the writings of the prophets. Passages like the following are typical:

When that day comes,

the mountains will run with new wine
and the hills flow with milk,
and all the river beds of Judah
will run with water (Joel 4:18).

The days are coming now –
it is the Lord who speaks –
when harvest will follow directly after ploughing,
the treading of grapes after sowing,
when the mountains will run with new wine
and the hills all flow with it.
I mean to restore the fortunes of my people Israel;
they will rebuild the ruined cities and live in them,
plant vineyards and drink their wine (Amos 9:13–14).

These yearnings are taken up and developed in a delightful
way in one of the latest writings of the Old Testament period.
The *Apocalypse of Baruch* speaks of the messianic days as a
time when each vine will have a thousand branches, and each
branch produce a thousand clusters, and each cluster contain a
thousand grapes, and each grape yield 120 gallons of wine!
Since this is precisely the amount of wine mentioned by John,
it is not difficult to hear the lyrical note he wishes to sound.
The same note is probably meant to be heard in his use of the
number six, a number which to people of his time would
denote incompleteness, since it falls short of the perfect
number seven. What Jesus brings into the world is a joy which
nothing preceding him was able to achieve.

The symbolism of wine is used in a number of the
'sapiential' writings of the Old Testament too, where divine
Wisdom (God's own double) issues his invitation to men in
words like these:

I am like a vine putting out graceful shoots . . .
Approach me you who desire me,
and take your fill of my fruits . . .
They who eat me will hunger for more,
they who drink me will thirst for more (Ecclesiasticus
    24:17–21).

Come all you who are thirsty;
even though you have no money, come!
Come and buy corn for nothing,
come and drink wine and milk at no cost . . .
Listen, listen to me,
and you will have good things to eat . . .
Pay attention, come to me;
listen, and your soul will live (Isaiah 55:1-3).

RE-READING THE STORY

All this, or at least something of this, ought to be in our minds
when we approach the story of Cana. That is the background
against which John wrote the story, and without some
familiarity with this Old Testament and New Testament
imagery and symbolism, expectation and hope, we will never
hear the rich overtones when we actually come to read the
story.

The messianic days have come, as all the Old Testament
promised they would. The Wisdom of God has come among
men, and taken up its dwelling among them. The marriage
between God and men, for which mankind has always longed,
has taken place. The 'old' dispensation – that is to say, any
religion which looks for communion with God in institutions
and customs, ritual and ceremonial – has been shown wanting;
it has run out, and must give place to the new and true worship
of God, in Spirit and truth, which can only take place in this
one person, in whom God is wedded for ever to mankind. And
so a transformation has taken place, the old into the new, the
incomplete into the complete, the ineffectual into the ef-
fectual, the imperfect into the perfect and life-giving, like
water into wine. Joy has come into the world, as when men
have their fill of corn and new wine, and there is no more room
for mourning and sour looks. A fullness and abundance has
been made available, and of that fullness we have all received.
The Glory of God has appeared among men, no longer in the
form of thunder and lightning but in the flesh and blood of
someone of our own race, and we have seen it and touched it.

When did all this happen? On the third day, when we realized that the water, which was all we could provide, had been changed into the blood of the grape. This was because the one who served it had taken on the position of a slave, because his Hour had come for his pass-over to his Father. And those who saw this were filled with a fullness they had never before experienced.

How does the reader of this story continue to experience this for himself? Through the wine which he continues to drink as it were from the very hands of Christ, where he recognizes both the blood of Jesus and the glory of God. Isn't it unreal, we may ask, to find a reference to something as recondite as the Christian eucharist in a story as simple as this? But isn't it unreal to imagine that a story about wine and crucifixion, written and read by people for whom the eucharist was a fact of their daily lives, could *fail* to have this reference?

WHAT ARE THE FACTS?

Some may feel that the preceding paragraphs are just so much poetry, and that it distracts them from the one question that bothers them: What really happened? Symbolism and allegory are all very well, but they feel like camouflage. What are the facts?

Such people should be warned that this hunger for facts can lead them astray. The facts we keep looking for are perhaps not to be found where we keep looking. The one fact underlying this story – it underlies all the stories of the New Testament – is the transformation brought about first of all in the body of Jesus at his death, and then in anyone who is granted the vision of that risen Christ and accepts to live by Christ's Spirit. Whoever has experienced such a transformation in himself knows that the story of Cana is 'true' without asking for further 'facts' to corroborate it. They are irrelevant. In the eyes of someone like John, or any Christian, who has experienced the resurrection of Jesus, the reality that occupies his attention as he tells or reads the story of Cana is that *on the third day there was a Marriage; Jesus was there; his Hour had come, and the water turned into Wine, the very best; and his disciples saw the Glory of God, and believed.*

All the stories told by John end with the word 'belief' or 'faith'. To believe in Jesus is not to believe that he can turn water into wine, like some heavenly magician. To believe in Jesus is to accept him as the one person who can replace our inadequate rituals of purification with the reality of union with God, in the wine of his own blood. In a later chapter, John is going to say this much more directly:

> Jesus cried out: 'If any man is thirsty, let him come to me!' . . . He was speaking of the Spirit which those who believed in him were to receive, and which would be given when he was glorified (7:38–9).

And the whole gospel will finish on the same note:

> These things have been written (not in order to keep a record of certain strange things that happened here recently, but) in order to nourish and sustain your faith in Jesus as the Christ and the Salvation of God (20:31).

4. Life to the Dying

(*John* 4–5)

John's gospel contains seven miracle stories. The fact that this book contains eight is due to the inclusion of the appendix to the gospel, of which more will be said below. The number seven would seem to be intentional. I mentioned above that seven was regarded as a 'round number', symbolic of totality and perfection, and the number is frequently used with this implication in the fourth gospel. There were numerous miracle stories available to him in the common tradition used by all four evangelists; he even makes passing allusion to them in 2:23, 3:2, 6:2, 7:31, 11:47, 20:30. If John has chosen to elaborate on just seven, it is presumably because he regarded these as providing a complete and comprehensive statement of what Jesus meant to him.

Two of the seven stories are less well known than the others, sandwiched as they are between three solid chapters of theological discourse. They deserve at least a short analysis, if only to indicate that they contain the same theological overtones as the other better known stories.

JOHN'S PLAN

John's gospel is carefully, indeed meticulously, planned (see p. 125 below). The 'prologue', as it is known (1:1–18), acts as a kind of table of contents, and announces the three themes with which the gospel is going to be concerned: 'In him was Life', 'That Life was the Light of men', and 'We saw his Glory'. After showing these three themes witnessed to by the first disciples (1:19–51) and illustrated in two concrete stories (Cana and the Temple, 2:1–25), the body of the gospel begins in chapter 3 by taking up the first of the themes, that of 'Life'. The theme will run through to the end of chapter 7.

What does it mean to say that Jesus is the Life? What sort of life are we talking about? Where is it that he becomes the source of that life to others, and how precisely do they share in it? These are the questions which John attempts to answer in the two discourses which occupy chapters 3 and 4 of his gospel, in the stories of Nicodemus and the Samaritan woman. And his answers are profound.

Jesus is the presence among men of the kind of life which God lives, life in all its fullness, unlimited by space and time, a life which in the last analysis is nothing other than self-giving love. This life will be made available 'when the Son of Man is lifted up' (3:14), to become as it were a bridge between heaven and earth. For from that exalted Christ will flow the 'Spirit' (3:5, 4:23, see 19:34) like lifegiving water to quench man's insatiable thirst (4:14). Man's part is to 'believe' (3:15), that is to say, to accept this crucified man as the 'truth' (4:24) – the unambiguous statement of what is ultimately real. This belief he will express in baptism (3:5, 4:14); it is there, John says, that the Christian receives the Spirit of the Son, whose exaltation on the cross has brought God's life into the world.

The two stories which follow these discourses are meant, as so often in John, to put this profound meditation into concrete form, to tie down to earth something which might tend for some readers to take flight into abstractions. The stories therefore mean what the discourses meant, they are 'signs' of the same reality, even if they are expressed in a different literary form.

JESUS THE LIFEGIVER

When the two days were over Jesus left for Galilee . . . He went again to Cana in Galilee, where he had changed the water into wine. Now there was a court official there whose son was ill at Capernaum and, hearing that Jesus had arrived in Galilee from Judaea, he went and asked him to come and cure his son as he was at the point of death. Jesus said, 'So you will not believe unless you see signs and portents!' 'Sir,' answered the official, 'come down before my child dies.' 'Go home,' said Jesus, 'your son will live.' The man believed what Jesus had said and started on his way; and while he was still on the journey back his servants met him with the news that his boy was alive. He asked them when the boy had begun to recover. 'The fever left him yesterday' they said 'at the seventh hour.' The father realized that this was exactly the time when Jesus had said, 'Your son will live'; and he and all his household believed. This was the second sign given by Jesus, on his return from Judaea to Galilee.

Some time after this there was a Jewish festival, and Jesus went up to Jerusalem. Now at the Sheep Pool in Jerusalem there is a building, called Bethzatha in Hebrew, consisting of five porticos; and under these were crowds of sick people – blind, lame, paralysed – waiting for the water to move. One man there had an illness which had lasted thirty-eight years, and when Jesus saw him lying there and knew he had been in this condition for a long time, he said, 'Do you want to be well again?' 'Sir,' replied the sick man 'I have no one to put me into the pool when the water is disturbed; and while I am still on the way, someone else gets there before me.' Jesus said, 'Get up, pick up your sleeping-mat and walk.' The man was cured at once, and he picked up his mat and walked away (John 4:43–5:9).

It was suggested above that the 'sign-value' or deeper meaning underlying John's apparently simple stories is to be discovered by digging out and analysing the clues he has buried in the stories. We shall follow the same procedure here.

The first of these clues is to be found in the setting of the two stories, one in Cana and the other in Jerusalem. The fact that the first two 'signs' in the gospel were similarly set in Cana and Jerusalem (2:1, 2:13) suggests that these two stories have the same meaning as the first two. Certainly John twice draws attention to the Cana parallelism in 4:46 and 54, and the phrase 'Jesus went up to Jerusalem' in 5:1 is a direct echo of 2:13. If those earlier stories are said to manifest the Glory, that is, to express in human terms the very reality of God, presumably these two stories do so too.

Both stories, therefore, like the story of the best wine of Cana and of the raised Temple of chapter 2, cast the reader's mind forward to Jesus' death and resurrection. The first story begins with the rubric 'when the two days were over' (4:43) which, though not a consecrated phrase like 'on the third day', is possibly meant to be an echo of it. The life-giving healing promised by Jesus is said to take effect at 'the seventh hour' (4:52), and the number seven is perhaps again used in the sense of 'complete', to suggest that fullness of life which Jesus was to give from his cross.

The timing of the second story is left imprecise: it was the time of 'a Jewish festival' (5:1). Some ancient manuscripts read 'the' instead of 'a', and this suggests the Passover festival, which would provide another link with Calvary. The location 'at the Sheep Pool' (5:2), though it is no doubt the name of a real reservoir, is possibly meant to evoke the later image of the Good Shepherd who brings life to his sheep by laying down his own (10:11). And the description of the cripple 'waiting for the water to flow' (5:4) – if indeed it is part of the original text: the manuscript evidence leaves some doubt – is probably a reference to the key-text of the whole gospel, in which John sees the water flowing from the side of the crucified Jesus as a symbol of the life-giving Spirit (7:39).

As at Calvary, the hopelessness of the situation, seen from a merely human point of view, is stressed. To the casual observer of Jesus' death, nothing could look less like God's salvation. Here too, the only thing that can be seen is death. The boy's predicament is desperate: he is slated to die. And the cripple too is as good as dead: he has been helpless for thirty-eight years, half a lifetime by any reckoning, a whole generation by Old Testament reckoning, stranded in an inescapable desert as hopelessly as his ancestors were when they awaited the fulfilment of God's promise (Deuteronomy 2:14 speaks of the Exodus lasting thirty-eight years). Possibly a further piece of symbolism is seen in the five porticos: the five volumes of the Jewish Law, even though they promise that healing is within striking distance, are in fact ineffective. As at Cana, the human situation has nothing to offer which could give any ground for hope.

In such a situation, the only adequate response is faith. That is what John is going to demand at Calvary, and he stresses it in these two stories too. Not a faith which demands miracles first – 4:48 expressly repudiates this – but an unconditional commitment to the power of God in Jesus: 'the man believed' (4:50); 'he and all his household believed' (4:53). When Matthew and Luke tell the story of the court official they underline even more strongly the kind of faith asked for here, faith such as Jesus had not encountered elsewhere (Matthew 8:10, Luke 7:9). Similarly the cripple cannot find healing without faith: '"Do you *want* to be well again? Get up." The man was cured at once' (John 5:7–8).

THE MEANING

The detailed clues analysed above are more ambiguous than those we have seen in the previous chapter and those we shall study below. Too much stress, therefore, should not be placed on them: there is always a danger of imposing on the text a pattern of our own choosing. But the argument does not depend on these details, rather on the whole context in which John has placed these miracle stories. In this context Jesus is being presented as the source of God's own life to men. The stories are not only preceded by two profound theological discourses, but followed by another, in which such statements as the following appear:

Jesus' answer to them was,
My Father goes on working, and so do I . . .
The Son can do nothing by himself;
he can only do what he sees the Father doing:
and whatever the Father does the Son does too . . .
Thus, as the Father raises the dead and gives them life,
so the Son *gives life* to anyone he chooses . . .
I tell you most solemnly,
whoever listens to my words,
and believes in the one who sent me,
has eternal life . . .
he *has* passed from death to life.
I tell you most solemnly,
the hour will come – in fact it is *here* already –

when the dead will hear the voice of the Son of God,
and all who hear it will live (John 5:17–25).

In this setting, our two stories are not simply accounts of the
remarkable healing powers men attributed to Jesus. They are
rich theological statements of what Jesus is for all believers at
all times. To resume these statements: To man in his helpless
condition, at death's door, God has sent his overwhelming life.
To man apparently hopeless in his desert exile, God fulfils the
promise he made. What the Law could not achieve because of
the frailty of our human situation, God has done by sending
his Son. On the third day, at the seventh hour of fulfilment,
when Jesus made his passover journey to his Father, the Good
Shepherd laid down his life to bring life to those who lay in the
shadow of death. And those who were waiting for the water to
flow recognized the Spirit which poured out of his pierced
side. Of that Spirit all those receive who believe in him, who
accept him as God's Word to men. Such faith is a transition
from death to life, a real sharing here and now in the
everlasting life that God lives. And the Christian expresses
this faith of his at the Pool of Water which is the baptismal
font.

Or, in the key words of the text, *When the two days were over,*
Jesus did what he had done at Cana. A boy was at the point of
death. Jesus said, 'He will have life. Will you believe even if there
are no signs and portents?' The father believed. The boy began to
recover at the seventh hour . . .

There was a Jewish festival, and Jesus went up to Jerusalem.
There crowds of people, like sick sheep, were waiting for the Water
to flow. One man there had an illness which had lasted for half a
lifetime. Jesus saw him lying there and knew that he had been in
this condition for a long time. He said, 'Do you want to be well?'
The sick man replied, 'I have no one to put me in the pool when the
Water flows.' Jesus said, 'Get up and walk.' The man was cured at
once.

44

5. Food in the Desert

(*John* 6)

Like the other chapters in this book, this chapter's treatment of the famous story of the loaves and fishes will be more of a meditation on the gospel narrative than a historical reconstruction of the event which lay behind the story. Others may ask historical questions if they wish; they are not of immediate concern to the evangelist.

This will mean, as elsewhere, resisting the temptation to adopt either of the two approaches which are often taken to the gospel miracle stories, approaches which are not on the whole very helpful.

UNHELPFUL APPROACHES

The approach most often taken to the miracle stories is the magical one: the miracle is simply something to astonish and stupefy. The child who wrote her own account of the first story in John's gospel and headed it 'The Magic Feast of Cana', had obviously been well schooled in this approach. So had the boy in the same class who described the story under discussion in this chapter as 'This was when Jesus turned five loaves and two fishes into five thousand men, not counting the women and children.' And indeed, if it is the weird and prodigious you are looking for, why not? Surely the weirder the better. I know a little girl who was allowed to go to Mass for the first time at the tender age of four, apparently well prepared with an explanation of what she was to see. She had to be taken out before the end in uncontrollable tears, and after much soothing sobbed out her reason, 'I never saw the priest turn into bread.' She has now happily outgrown the magical fantasies of her childhood. In matters religious, many adults never do.

At the opposite extreme is the sweetly reasonable approach, which simply makes a few 'minor' adjustments to the story to remove all difficulties from it. In the case under discussion, for instance, the Essene community living by the Dead Sea had left an enormous stock of bread in a hole in the ground, and Jesus was simply standing over the hole fetching out the loaves as they were required. Or, the story has become a little exaggerated in the telling; the crowd numbered only a few hundred (not five thousand), and there were probably about fifty loaves (not five), so they easily went round. Or, what really happened was that Jesus shared his own bread, and this shamed others into digging out the sandwiches they had kept hidden, until plenty was found for everyone. Or, what really happened was that Jesus spoke words so moving that no one noticed they had eaten only a few crumbs each: it felt just like a full meal.

These 'solutions' to the story have their interest, and I would not wish simply to dismiss them out of hand even though they apparently remove every element of mystery. However, our first interest should be that of the evangelist. We should ask with him: 'What does this story mean when told to people who have experienced the same Jesus die and rise in glory?'

LOAVES AND FISHES

Jesus went off to the other side of the Sea of Galilee – or of Tiberias – and a large crowd followed him, impressed by the signs he gave by curing the sick. Jesus climbed the hillside, and sat down there with his disciples. It was shortly before the Jewish feast of Passover.

Looking up, Jesus saw the crowds approaching and said to Philip, 'Where can we buy some bread for these people to eat?' He only said this to test Philip; he himself knew exactly what he was going to do. Philip answered, 'Two hundred denarii would only buy enough to give them a small piece each.' One of his disciples, Andrew, Simon Peter's brother, said, 'There is a small boy here with five barley loaves and two fish; but what is that between so many?' Jesus said to them, 'Make the people sit down.' There was plenty of grass there, and as many as five thousand men sat down. Then

Jesus took the loaves, gave thanks, and gave them out to all who were sitting ready; he then did the same with the fish, giving out as much as was wanted. When they had eaten enough he said to the disciples, 'Pick up the pieces left over, so that nothing gets wasted.' So they picked them up, and filled twelve hampers with scraps left over from the meal of five barley loaves. The people, seeing this sign that he had given, said, 'This really is the prophet who is to come into the world.' Jesus, who could see that they were about to come and take him by force and make him king, escaped back to the hills by himself (John 6:1–15).

The principal theme of the story is the one which formed the background to the story of Cana, the theme of a meal or banquet. When Jesus said, in his Sermon on the Mount, 'Blessed are the hungry, they shall have their fill', he was not inventing new imagery. He was taking up a commonplace which prophets, psalmists and Wisdom writers had used to express the idea of Kingdom Come. God's Kingdom, or man's yearned-for union with God, could be compared to the happiness and joy of a meal where the hunger of starved men is satisfied. The theme was illustrated above with quotations from Joel, Amos, Ecclesiasticus and Isaiah. Texts such as the following could be added:

> On this mountain of Zion
> the Lord of hosts will prepare for all peoples
> a banquet of rich food, a banquet of fine wines,
> of food rich and juicy, of fine strained wines.
> On this mountain he will remove
> the mourning veil covering all peoples,
> and the shroud enwrapping all nations,
> he will destroy Death for ever (Isaiah 25:6–8).

> Wisdom has built herself a house,
> she has erected her seven pillars,
> she has slaughtered her beats, prepared her wine,
> she has laid her table.
> She has despatched her maidservants

47

and proclaimed from the city heights:
'Who is without wisdom? Let him step this way.'
To the unwise she says,
'Come and eat my bread,
Drink the wine I have prepared' (Proverbs 9:1–5).

Jesus took up the imagery more than once. Even outside his wedding parables, he compared the Kingdom to a banquet to which people would come from east and west, to sit down at the same table as Abraham, Isaac and Jacob (Matthew 8:11). To say that the hungry are fed, that the poor do not have to pay, and that there is bread enough for all comers – this is to say that the Kingdom of God has come among men. That is certainly the main theme in this story of a meal where no one went hungry.

LOOKING FOR CLUES

For more specific clues a closer examination of the text is needed. The margin of an annotated bible will point out that the question put by Jesus, and Philip's cynical reply, are intended to remind the reader of the story of the desert exodus in the book of Numbers. Jesus asks here, 'Where can we buy bread for these people to eat?' just as Moses asked there, 'Where am I to find food to give to all this people?' (Numbers 11:13). And Philip's reply here, 'A year's wage would just about give everyone a nibble' is an echo of the reply there, 'If we slaughtered all the flocks and herds, and gathered all the fish in the sea, it would still not be enough' (Numbers 11:22).

In the exodus story, these remarks form the prelude to the account of the providential food obtained by Moses for the desert march. And on his deathbed Moses prays that God will appoint someone who can continue to act as shepherd for this people, and find pasture for them (Numbers 27:15). When Mark 6:34 tells the story, he draws explicit attention to this parallelism.

As Israel's precarious desert phase gave way to the security of the monarchy, the same figure of speech is still to be found to express the continued need for a shepherd and provider. In one of the psalms God is represented as making David this oath:

> I promise you your own son
> will succeed you on the throne . . .
> I will bless your people with riches,
> and provide your poor with bread (Psalm 132:11, 15).

When finally the story of Israel's kings opens on to the story of the prophets, the theme is arrestingly illustrated in one of the Elisha sagas:

> A man came from Baal-shalishah, bringing the man of God bread from the first-fruits, twenty barley loaves . . . 'Give it to the people to eat', Elisha said. But his servant replied, 'How can I serve this to a hundred men?' 'Give it to the people to eat' he insisted 'for the Lord says this, "They will eat and have some left over".' He served them; they ate and had some left over, as the Lord had said (2 Kings 4:42–4).

It is these or similar texts which John seems to have in mind when he tells the story of the loaves and fishes. He wants to present Jesus not merely as the one who brings the Kingdom in general, but specifically as a new Moses feeding the multitudes in the desert, a new Joshua leading his flock to pasture, a new David in whose time the poor are fed, a new Elisha in whose hands the barley loaves multiply. In short, John is saying that Jesus is the messiah, the culmination of all the great figures of Israel's past. This is the conclusion arrived at – even in the story – by the crowd, who wish to seize him and proclaim him king, convinced that he is the one 'who is to come'. The word used was one of the official titles then in use for the messiah.

IRRELEVANT DETAILS?

How does John envisage Jesus becoming messiah, or establishing himself as messiah, or manifesting his messianic claim? The answer lies in the opening line of the story: 'It was shortly before the Jewish feast of Passover.'

Some commentators, supposing that it would have made no difference whether this event took place at Easter or Christmas, ask why John should include such an irrelevant detail. They come to the naïve conclusion that John must have been getting old, with an old man's annoying habit of interspersing his reminiscences with useless information. But John's little finger is thicker than the loins of most commentators, and if he mentions a Passover it is more than likely that it had significance for him.

It is not only the first Passover he wants to evoke, as the references to Moses and the manna make clear. He has in mind, above all, the Easter Passover which was to come, when Jesus would take bread and give thanks (literally, as in the story under discussion, 'make eucharist'), and explicitly make of that a symbol of his death and resurrection. What John is evoking above all in his telling of the story is Jesus' glorification through death: that is the moment when Jesus became the new Moses, the new Joshua, the new David, the new Elisha, the moment when he brought about Kingdom Come. Matthew and Mark, in their telling of the story, speak of the crowds being foodless in the desert for three days before having their hunger assuaged.

It is worth remarking again what unlikely material goes into the making of that glory. Cana was able to offer an amount of tasteless water, that's all. Chapters 4 and 5 presented us with a boy and a man as good as dead, that's all. Here we have five barley loaves, that's all. It is out of this unpromising material, this human nothingness, that God works such wonders that at the end there is more left over than there was to start with.

The meaning of the story, therefore, in its key words, is that *Jesus climbed the hillside, about the time of Passover; he satisfied the hunger of thousands from apparently nothing; they recognized the sign that he had given them; and they said, 'This really is the One who is to come.'*

Is there perhaps a danger that we are reading too much into the story? Would it not be more reasonable to suppose that the story simply means what it says, and that all this talk of Kingdom Come and messianic expectations, of manna and divine Wisdom, of Passover and Jesus' death and resurrection, is far too sophisticated to be part of a story as simple as that of the loaves and fishes?

Anyone worried on that score need do nothing more than read on a little further in this chapter of John's gospel. Like the stories in chapters 4 and 5, only much more explicitly, the story of the loaves and fishes has attached to it a discourse, this time fifty verses long, where all the themes touched on above are opened out. The reader can be left in no doubt that the miracle story was intended to have precisely those overtones. Why tell a story of Jesus feeding the multitudes? Because Jesus himself, through his death and resurrection, has in his own person become the satisfaction of all men's hunger.

This discourse should therefore be examined if the story is to be understood in depth. We shall again, in our examination, leave aside such historical questions as, Where were these words spoken? At what stage in Jesus' ministry? Why? To what sort of audience? How were they received? What is the connection between one part of the discourse and the next? We simply do not know the answers to such questions, nor is there any reason why the discourse as it now stands should not be the amalgamation of several independent pieces. The only question we can answer with some degree of confidence is, What would this discourse mean to someone who accepts the Jesus who died as his living Lord? It is on this question, therefore, that we shall concentrate. We shall omit, at a first reading, the explicitly 'eucharistic' verses in order to deal with them on their own afterwards. The discourse as it stands has a much wider reference than the eucharist. John insists that it is for all men, not only for communicants, that Jesus is the heaven-sent food without which they will die in the desert.

Next day, the crowd that had stayed on the other side . . . crossed to Capernaum to look for Jesus. When they found him on the other side, they said to him, 'Rabbi, when did you come here?' Jesus answered:

'I tell you most solemnly,
you are not looking for me
because you have understood the signs
but because you had all the bread you wanted to eat.
Do not work for food that cannot last,
but work for food that endures to eternal life,
the kind of food the Son of Man is offering you,
for on him the Father, God himself, has set his seal.'

Then they said to him, 'What must we do if we are to do the works that God wants?' Jesus gave them this answer, 'This is working for God: you must believe in the one he has sent.' So they said, 'What sign will you give to show us that we should believe in you? What work will you do? Our fathers had manna to eat in the desert; as scripture says: "He gave them bread from heaven to eat".

Jesus answered:

'I tell you most solemnly,
it was not Moses who gave you bread from heaven,
it is my Father who give you the bread from heaven,
the true bread;
for the bread of God
is that which comes down from heaven
and gives life to the world.'

'Sir,' they said 'give us that bread always.' Jesus answered:

'I am the bread of life.
He who comes to me will never be hungry;
he who believes in me will never thirst . . .'

The Jews were complaining to each other about him, because he had said, 'I am the bread that came down from heaven.' 'Surely this is Jesus son of Joseph' they said. 'We know his father and mother. How can he now say, "I have come down from heaven"?' Jesus said in reply:

> 'Stop complaining to each other . . .
> I am the bread of life.
> Your fathers ate the manna in the desert
> and they are dead;
> but this is the bread that comes down from heaven,
> so that a man may eat it and not die' (John 6:22–50).

It is significant that the discourse begins with an explicit disclaimer of the approach that is normally taken to the miracle story, as if it were merely, or mainly, a physical marvel which provided food for hungry bellies. To stay at that material level, says John, is to miss the whole point. For John, the story about bread has been mainly a symbol for the *real* food, food which will never fail, food which is genuinely God-given, food which produces life in all its fullness, food which surpasses even the exodus manna. Mann, for all its 'heavenly' origin, had only an earthly purpose; it could never finally insure anyone against death. Whatever kind of bread the reader might have been thinking of in the story of the loaves, for John it has only been an opportunity for thinking about the real Bread, the nourishment which is death-proof because it continues to give life even after death. And this Bread is Jesus himself, not only in the eucharist, but more fundamentally in his own person. He *is* the Bread of Life.

FEEDING ON CHRIST

How is this Bread to be eaten? In what way are we to 'feed on' Christ? The same question is asked in the discourse when Jesus tells his listeners to 'work for the food which endures to eternal life': 'What must we *do* if we are to do the works which God wants?' The answer is:

This is working for God:
you must *believe* in the one he has sent . . .
He who comes to me will never be hungry,
he who *believes* in me will never thirst.

The way in which Christ is to be assimilated, the way in which union with Christ is to be achieved, the way in which a person is to drink in Christ and live on him, is by the commitment of faith.

There is a finality about such a commitment. The Old Testament invitation to take one's fill of divine Wisdom has already been quoted:

They who eat me will hunger for more,
they who drink me will thirst for more. (Ecclesiasticus 24:21)

When John says that anyone who eats and drinks of Christ will never hunger or thirst again, he is pointing to the climax of this theme, beyond which it is impossible to go. Moses had only mediated the gift of God: Jesus is the gift. Moses had only spoken the word of God: Jesus is that Word embodied in the life of a man.

And since the question must naturally occur, 'How does Jesus become such a life-giving food? How is he made available for us to assimilate him? When does our faith become an eating which nourishes us?' the discourse reaches its culmination in its closing lines:

After hearing this, many of his followers said, 'This is intolerable language. How could anyone accept it?' Jesus was aware that his followers were complaining about it and said, 'Does this upset you? What if you should see the Son of man ascend to where he was before?

It is the Spirit that gives life,
the flesh has nothing to offer' (John 6: 60–3).

Throughout his gospel John uses the word 'ascent' of Jesus'

death on the cross. For John, the scene at Calvary represents not only the lowest moment in Jesus' life – in one sense it was that too – but above all its highpoint. The crucifixion is truly his exaltation, his lifting up, the moment when he is raised above our poor earth and is already, as it were, on his way into the heavens. John does not therefore distinguish, as we usually do, between death, resurrection, ascension and pentecost. For him they are all one. Jesus' crucifixion is already his ascent into heaven; from his dying mouth he breathes out his Spirit, and from his pierced side flows the water which is a sign of that Spirit.

That is why 'the flesh' has nothing to offer: man insofar as he is devoid of God can only sink by his own weight into eternal death. It is only the Spirit that can give life: the divine life of which this chapter has been speaking is only available when Jesus' body of flesh has been transformed into a body of Spirit, and he is able to pour out the Spirit on all who believe in him. The death, resurrection, ascension and pentecost of Jesus form the centre of the mystery that makes him the Christ. This is how he becomes for all believers the Bread of Life.

BODY AND BLOOD

To understand this discourse at its deepest level we must turn finally to the verses we have not yet commented on. They stand in a central position in the discourse. Even though they continue to speak in general of Jesus as the Bread of Life, they form a unit of their own. This is clear not only from the *inclusio* whereby the closing line repeats the words of the opening line, but from a distinct shift of emphasis. Here the Bread is given no longer by the Father but by Jesus; it is eaten no longer 'metaphorically' but in reality; and it is identified no longer with the person of Jesus in general but specifically with his body and blood. The passage runs as follows:

I am the living bread which has come down from heaven.
Anyone who eats this bread will live for ever;
and the bread that I shall give

is my flesh, for the life of the world . . .
I tell you most solemnly,
if you do not eat the flesh of the Son of Man
and drink his blood,
you will not have life in you.
Anyone who does eat my flesh and drink my blood
has eternal life,
and I shall raise him up on the last day.
For my flesh is real food
and my blood is real drink.
He who eats my flesh and drinks my blood
lives in me and I live in him.
As I, who am sent by the living Father,
myself draw life from the Father,
so whoever eats me will draw life from me.
This is the bread come down from heaven;
not like the bread our ancestors ate:
they are dead,
but anyone who eats this bread
will live for ever (John 6:51–58).

Most New Testament scholars agree – some to the extent that they regard this section as a later addition to John's gospel – that in these verses the thought has moved from the general theme of faith in Jesus to the specific theme of the Christian eucharist. This view is confirmed firstly by the repeated emphasis on the word 'to eat': twice the author uses an almost brutal word in the Greek, 'to feed on, to chew, to get one's teeth into'. But secondly and more especially by the close parallelism between the words used here and the words of institution to be found in the other gospels, 'This bread is my body which is given for you.'

It comes as a surprise to many readers of the gospel that John has no record of the institution of the eucharist in his account of Jesus' last supper. It is probable that he means us to find a reference to the supper in the words he records here, 'The bread that I shall give is my flesh which is for the life of the world.' The parallelism would be even stronger in Aramaic, which has no separate word for 'body' and 'flesh'.

We have seen that the story of the wine at Cana must have evoked the thought of the eucharist for John's communicating readers. Here too anyone in the year 100 AD reading of Jesus as the Bread of Life could not help thinking of his holy communion.

What is interesting about the shift of emphasis represented in these verses is that the original author should have felt it quite normal to weave a specifically eucharistic theme into a general discourse about faith in Christ. It suggests that many Christians distinguish too readily between the faith and the eucharist which unites them to Christ. By making such a rigid distinction between them they finish up with a stunted view of both eucharist and faith.

UNDERPLAYING THE EUCHARIST

We get a stunted view of the eucharist if we look only at this section of the discourse which refers explicitly to the eucharist. The rest of the discourse, we think, is not on that topic, and so in dealing with the eucharist we need not refer to it.

Yet John, by interleaving the eucharistic verses with the rest, has implicitly told us that the rest of the chapter is about the eucharist too. The Christian is being invited to read the whole chapter, not just these few verses, to understand that it is precisely in his holy communion that he assists at the messianic banquet and is fed on his way through the desert to God's Kingdom. It is in the eucharist that the deepest hunger and yearning of his heart will be satisfied, as he is given a share in the immortal life of God himself. It is in communion that he is invited to accept Jesus' way of self-sacrifice as the only way which will give meaning to his own life, and is asked to abandon himself utterly to Christ in faith. These themes are all developed in the 'non-eucharistic' parts of the discourse. John has wrapped them around the 'eucharistic' part to tell us that they too are relevant to the eucharist.

The same is true, of course, of all the other chapters of the gospel. What the Christian is meant to experience at communion is not simply what happened at the last supper. His communion is meant to draw him into the mystery of Cana and of the cleansing of the temple; of the walking on the water, the healing of the blind man and the raising of Lazarus; of the anointing at Bethany, the condemnation by Pilate and the death on Calvary; of the appearance to Mary in the garden, the promise to the disciples on the first Easter evening and the meal on the lakeside. The Christian takes part in all these events at communion because communion unites him to Christ, and he is the mystery expressed in all these stories.

If we separate the eucharist from our faith in what Christ is, we underplay the eucharist.

UNDERPLAYING FAITH

But equally, we must not dissociate faith from the eucharist, otherwise we underplay the value of and the need for faith.

There are many Christians who do this, when they speak, for instance, of being united to Christ *really* in holy communion but only *metaphorically* in faith, as if this was not also a real union with him. They forget that John himself does not hesitate to put these two ways of union with Christ in exact parallel with each other. John presents Jesus speaking to people who have no notion of the eucharist in exactly the same way that he speaks of the eucharist to communicating Christians. Because for those others too he is the Food without which they will die, and they too 'eat' him when they accept his word in faith.

Both faith and eucharist unite us to the same Christ in all his reality, body, blood, soul and divinity. The service of the Word which precedes communion should be, and can be, as true a communion with Christ as the eucharist itself. The noted French theologian, Yves Congar, envisages the situation of two communities, of which one has the eucharist without the Word of God, and the other the Word of God without the eucharist. After a period of twenty years, he asks, which of the two would be more truly Christian? He himself opts firmly for the second. The fact that this suggestion has angered some sacramental Christians indicates the extent to which they have separated their faith from their communion.

At its deepest level, this chapter of John's gospel warns us to beware of disassociating the eucharist and faith. The eucharist does not somehow stand on its own, outside the area of faith. The effect of the eucharist is not automatic but requires faith. Christ is not more present to the tabernacle than he is to us because he stays there longer. Holy communion has to do with a presence of Christ which is personal, and which is therefore meaningless without faith. Christ is not present 'in' the tabernacle in the same way as he is present 'to' us. Tabernacles do not derive any benefit from the presence of Christ. Christ is not in love with boxes, but with people.

6. Walking on the Water

(*John* 6)

There is yet another section of John 6 which, in our selective reading, we have not yet considered. It contains another miracle story, the fifth of John's series of seven.

> That evening the disciples went down to the shore of the lake and got into a boat to make for Capernaum on the other side of the lake. It was getting dark by now and Jesus had still not rejoined them. The wind was strong, and the sea was getting rough. They had rowed three or four miles when they saw Jesus walking on the lake and coming towards the boat. 'This frightened them, but he said, 'It is I. Do not be afraid.' They were for taking him into the boat, but in no time it reached the shore at the place they were making for (6:16–21).

PUTTING IT IN CONTEXT

Faced with this story, many will immediately want to ask, 'Did it happen just like that?' It is not a very helpful question, since the answer to it depends very much on one's world picture, one's view of what is and what is not within the bounds of physical possibility. And when the question leads to speculations about whether the law of gravity can at the same time be in operation (to allow one foot to be placed in front of the other) and suspended (to allow a literal walking on the water), one appreciates the wisdom of the saying, 'Ask a silly question.'

I have already suggested many times that the only fruitful question we may ask of the miracles stories, as indeed of any page of the gospel, is, 'What did this mean when told or heard by someone who had seen the risen Christ?' If all the gospel stories are told in the light of Jesus' death and resurrection, then that is the first reality they are intended to evoke. Read in that context, the story of the walking on the water takes on all the overtones of the resurrection scenes with which the gospel narrative closes. Certain key phrases are common: 'They were afraid', 'Jesus came and stood among them', 'Do not be afraid; it is not a ghost, it is I.' Indeed, one has only to put onself inside the skin of one of the apostles after the apparent débâcle of Calvary to recognize what such a story would mean for him, in its key sentences: *That evening the disciples went down to the sea. It was getting dark, and Jesus had still not rejoined them. The wind was strong, and the sea was getting rough. They had gone some distance when they saw Jesus walking on the water and coming towards them. This frightened them, but he said, 'It is I. Do not be afraid.' And in no time they reached the shore.*

LOOKING FOR CLUES

That Jesus' unexpected resurrection is the principal theme of this story emerges even more clearly when the clue offered by the word 'sea' is recognized. For a seafaring nation like Britain the word can only conjure up adventure, exploration and challenge. But the Palestine seaboard offers no natural harbours and the Jews, who never possessed a navy, felt constantly threatened by the ravenous sea that stretched the length of their coastline. They looked forward to heaven as a place where 'there will be no more sea' (Revelation 21:1). Others before me have pointed out that the only two seafarers of theirs who ever became famous, Paul and Jonah, were both thrown overboard.

In this context, from the very first page of the bible, the sea represents the hostile and chaotic element which God has to overcome if he is to establish an ordered universe fit for men to live in. This sinister meaning of 'sea', even of an inland sea, runs through the stories of the exodus from Egypt, where the sea is the death-dealing element from which God rescues his son Israel. It runs through the psalter's cries for help from those who find themselves in the 'depths' from which God alone can save them, the Lord who is 'on the immensity of waters'.

The following quotations from the Old Testament will establish the feeling that sea and deep water must have evoked in a Jew like John:

In the beginning . . .
there was darkness over the deep,
and God's Spirit hovered over the water . . .
God said, 'Let there be a vault
to divide the waters in two.'
God made the vault,
and it divided the waters above the vault
from the waters under the vault . . .
God said, 'Let the waters under heaven
come together into a single mass,
and let dry land appear.'
And so it was.
God called the dry land 'earth'
and the mass of waters 'seas'.
And God saw that it was good (Genesis 1:1–10).

Who pent up the sea behind closed doors when it leapt
    tumultuous out of the womb,
when I wrapped it in a robe of mist and made black
    clouds its swaddling bands;
when I marked the bounds it was not to cross and made
    it fast with a bolted gate?
Come thus far, I said, and no farther: here your proud
    waves shall break (Job 38:8–11).

You control the pride of the ocean,
when its waves ride high, you calm them;
you split the monster in two like a carcase
and scattered your enemies with your mighty arm (Psalm
    89:9–10).

When the waters saw it was you, God,
when the waters saw it was you, they recoiled,
shuddering to their depths,.

The clouds poured down water,
the sky thundered,
your arrows darted out.
Your thunder crashed as it rolled,
your lightning lit up the world,
the earth shuddered and quaked.
You strode across the sea,
you marched across the ocean,
but your steps could not be seen.
You guided your people like a flock
by the hands of Moses and Aaron (Psalm 77:16–20).

If the Lord had not been on our side . . .
the waters would have closed over us,
the torrent have swept us away,
either would have drowned us
in their turbulent waves (Psalm 124:2–5).

The waves of death encircled me . . .
the cords of the Underworld girdled me,
the snares of death were before me . . .
The bed of the seas was revealed,
the foundations of the world were laid bare,
at your muttered threat, o Lord,
at the blast of your nostrils' breath.
He sends from on high and takes me,
he draws me from deep waters (Psalm 18:4–16).

In your great love, answer me, God . . .
save me from deep water!
Do not let the waves wash over me,
do not let the deep swallow me
or the Underworld close its mouth on me (Psalm
    69:13–15).

In short, the sea is the unmasterable element, the destroyer. It
is the mouth of the Underworld, the home of the great Beast
who lurks like the Loch Ness Monster seeking whom he may
devour. What must be conjured up by picturing one who *walks*
on the sea, as its master!

Jesus went into that abode of death. God drew him out of death, to establish him as its master. The one who had apparently fallen asleep, who had, it seemed, succumbed to death like the rest of mortals, was roused from that sleep to be manifested as its Lord. When Matthew tells of the storm at sea (8:26) he speaks of Jesus being 'aroused', and it is the same word as the one used for the 'raising up' of Jesus in the resurrection accounts.

In Matthew's account of the walking on the water, Jesus is not the only one who masters the elements. Peter, by recognizing him, finds that he is able to do so too. He does so hesitantly at first, and in great danger of being sucked under by the unfamiliar element; his question, 'Lord, if it *is* you' could be translated '*Is* the crucified Jesus alive for me, or now only a ghost from the Underworld?' But he survives in the knowledge that Jesus has not been swallowed up by death. Peter discovered, and it is this witness of his which confirmed the faith of his brethren, that Jesus is the unsinkable one, more powerful than the death that stalks all men, and that he summons each man to come to him across the waters of death. Faith is nothing other than that, a putting of one's hand in the hand of the man who walked the water, in order to live, as he did, in the midst of death. The closing story of John's gospel has kept some traces of this vivid imagery (see chapter 9 below).

WHAT REALLY HAPPENED?

What precise historical facts, apart from Jesus' death and resurrection, lie behind the story of the walking on the water, it is difficult to say. There have been many attempts to make the story sweetly reasonable and 'inherently credible', for instance by suggesting that Jesus was not really walking on the sea but only on the sea-*side*, and appeal is made to the English usage of 'St Anne's-*on*-Sea' to give this some plausibility. But while such a suggestion is commendable as an attempt to make the gospel speak to people who are shy of miracles, it is ruinous to the *story* – even more as Matthew and Mark recount it. The story *demands* something 'impossible', otherwise there is no point in telling it, least of all in John, where it interrupts the orderly telling of the story of the loaves and fishes.

At the same time it is difficult to understand why John makes so little of the story, with not even a discourse to elaborate on it. Why does he not make the references to the resurrection even plainer, as Matthew's gospel does, where the disciples at first mistake Jesus for a ghost, and then explicitly profess their Easter faith in him as the Son of God? Why does John locate the event not in the most dangerous part of the sea, but apparently near land so that 'in no time they reached the shore'? Why does John omit the telling detail of Peter's courage in trying to walk on the sea? To these questions we have no answers. It is simply no longer possible for us to put our finger on the event in Galilee which first gave rise to the story.

It is equally difficult to tell any longer what precise historical fact lies behind the story of the loaves and fishes. The late C. H. Dodd, by carefully comparing all the accounts in the four gospels, suggests that it may have had a political background. The crowds were trying to inveigle Jesus into supporting the cause of those first-century muscle-men who called themselves Zealots. Jesus diplomatically refused their offer of kingship by inviting them all to share a *symbolic* meal. In such a meal, as in holy communion, a little bread can go a long way. He was saying, in effect, that the revolution he stood for was one in which the Kingdom was here and now available in men's union with each other and with God. The traditional account of the event ended with the words, 'They understood not about the loaves', meaning no more than that nobody saw the point of it at the time. But it is a phrase which possibly gave the rest of the story an air of mystery, and caused it to be told as if it were something awesome, hence spectacular, when the original event may not have been spectacular at all (*The Founder of Christianity*, Collins, London, 1971 pp. 133–5). It is a reasonable hypothesis.

A more familiar reconstruction of the event is along the lines suggested earlier, namely that the five thousand were easily fed because they were all shamed by Jesus' example into sharing with their neighbours the food they had brought with them. This 'explanation' is often summarily dismissed as sheer rationalism, an attempt to avoid the supernatural. But it at least tries to put some positive significance into a story which would be pointless otherwise. After all, which has more meaning, the supernatural multiplication of bread two thousand years ago, or the call to men to share here and now what they have with others? Which would anyone rather do, if he had the power, multiply a number of loaves or move all men to be more sharing of themselves? Which is more likely to solve the problems of the world we live in?

The truth is, however, that since the gospel is the kind of document it is, it no longer allows us to pinpoint the precise 'facts' which lie behind the miracle stories. Or, more accurately, it allows us to pinpoint the all-important fact which lies behind them all, which is the death and resurrection of Jesus. It was in that event that Jesus was recognized to be the Christ whom the waters of death could not destroy, the Bread which God has sent among men to satisfy their eternal hunger, and the living Lord who is the giver of Life.

7. Sight to the Blind

(John 9)

The sixth of John's seven miracle stories tells of the healing of the man born blind. It looks at first like a very simple story: Jesus puts some mud on a blind man's eyes, who washes it off to see for the first time, and then engages in a glorious battle of words with the authorities. Yet when the story is examined closely it turns out to be the concentrated essence of many pages of high-powered theology. The story of the blind man in chapter 9 is in fact only part of a long sequence stretching from chapter 7 to chapter 10. To be faithful to our author we must be prepared to roam about those chapters. They provide the context in which this apparently simple tale is to be understood, and reveal its meaning.

TABERNACLES

Chapter 7 begins with the words, 'The Jewish feast of Tabernacles drew near.' This is as significant a rubric as the one on the feast of Passover which introduced the story of the loaves and fishes and gave a clue to its meaning. We need to know something about the feast of Tabernacles in order to understand the story of the man born blind.

Tabernacles remains one of the three great annual Jewish feast-days. In Jesus' time a good Jew would try to go on pilgrimage to Jerusalem. It fell in the autumn and was originally a harvest festival. But in the course of Israel's history it eventually became a commemoration of the desert journey from Egypt to Palestine, and the feast was thought of as completing the Passover with which the desert journey began. The pilgrims coming to Jerusalem would collect branches and make 'tabernacles' or huts around the city. In these they would live for the week so that they could attend the daily ceremonies on Temple hill.

The ceremonies were centred around two themes: water and

light. The water theme was expressed in prayers for rain. Every day of the week there was a procession down the southern end of Temple hill to Siloam, the pool formed by the underground aqueduct of water 'sent' there from Jerusalem's only water water supply higher up the valley outside the city. Buckets of water were brought back from Siloam and carried up the hill to be poured out on the altar in the Temple, where the Hallel psalms were sung with the antiphon from Isaiah 12:3, 'You will draw water with joy from the fountain of salvation.' The final day, known as the Great Day, concluded with the most solemn prayers for the rain needed for the coming year. Even travellers had to bow before the common need, and God was asked not to listen to their prayers for fine weather.

The theme of light was also expressed in a daily ceremony. The whole of the outer court of the Temple, open to the sky, was fitted with twelve immense candelabra. These were lit every evening of the week and kept burning all night. It is said that one could see this blaze of light for miles around. The candles illuminated the whole city, turning it into Jerusalem the Golden, and extending as it were an invitation to all men to come to this source of light. Then each morning, as the dawn broke and the fires died out to give way to the first rays of the sun on the Temple, the priests would come out from their inner court, march through the outer court to the eastern edge of the Temple area, turn round to face the Temple, and point to it as the dwelling place of God, the Light of the World. On this occasion the antiphon used was taken from Psalm 27:1, 'The Lord is my light and my saviour, whom shall I fear?' So this original harvest festival became a great yearning for the final harvest, when all men would find the true God on Temple hill.

Both these themes, of the water of Siloam and of darkness giving way to light, form part of the story of the man born blind. They also form part of the preaching of Jesus with which John prefaces the story:

On the last day of the festival, the Great Day, Jesus stood there and cried out:

68

'If any man is thirsty, let him come to me!
Let the man come and drink who believes in me!'

As scripture says: From his breast shall flow fountains of living water. He was speaking of the Spirit which those who believed in him were to receive; for the Spirit had not yet been given because Jesus had not yet been glorified (John 7:37–9).

At daybreak he appeared in the Temple again; and as all the people came to him, he sat down and began to teach them . . . He said:

I am the light of the world;
anyone who follows me
will not be walking in the dark;
he will have the light of life' (John 8:2, 12).

This is the rich theological area which John is inviting us to enter as he prepares to tell his story of the man born blind. We have already twice accompanied him into the Wisdom literature to contemplate with him the depths he sees in Jesus. Here he has aptly gone to the same books again to give us an allusion to the text:

On the hilltop, Wisdom takes her stand . . .
and beside the gates of the city she cries aloud,
'O men! I am calling to you' . . .
Wisdom proclaims from the city's heights . . .
'Come and eat my bread
drink the wine I have prepared!' (Proverbs 8:2–4,
    9:3–5).

For John, Jesus is the Wisdom of God become flesh and blood, the source of eternal life. He is the true Temple from which issues a stream to irrigate the whole earth, and the stream begins to flow when his side is opened.

The theme of light must be opened out a little more to clarify John's thought. Basically, to call Jesus the Light of the World is to say that he is the messiah, the fulfilment of Israel's hopes for the age to come. The hope is expressed when the word is used of the Suffering Servant:

> I have appointed you as covenant of the people
> and light of the nations,
> to open the eyes of the blind . . .
> I will make you the light of the nations
> so that my salvation may reach
> to the ends of the earth (Isaiah 42:6–7, 49:6)

Earlier the hoped-for ideal king of the future is spoken of in the same terms:

> The people that walked in darkness
> have seen a great light;
> on those who live in a land of deep shadow
> a light has shone (Isaiah 9:1).

The theme is taken up in the New Testament where Zechariah also looks forward to one who will

> give light to those who live
> in darkness and the shadow of death (Luke 1:79).

Simeon too says he is willing to die now that his eyes have seen

> a light to enlighten the pagans
> and the glory of your people Israel (Luke 2:32).

But the messiah is never thought of as being a light in his own right. The light he brings is only a reflection of God. God alone is the true light. John will later express this with some force in his epistle:

This is the message we are announcing to you:
God is light;
there is no darkness in him at all.
If we say that we are in union with God
while we are living in darkness,
we are lying! (1 John 1:5–6).

And this figure of speech is to be found frequently throughout the Old Testament. Light is thought of as a correlative to life, which is impossible without light. To live is to be 'in the light'; to die is 'to be snuffed out, to be switched off, to go into the darkness'. Light is a natural symbol of life, as darkness is of death. And if life only comes to men as a gift from the living God, so light originates in the God who is light.

So the oldest Israelite traditions spoke of God in terms of a pillar of fire or a luminous cloud leading the forefathers through the desert. And the later traditions spoke of the *Kabhod* or Glory, blinding and inaccessible. Ezekiel's vision of the Chariot of God is something he finds it well nigh impossible to describe, so dazzled is he by its brightness (Ezekiel 1:4–28). And Daniel's vision of the Ancient of Days can similarly only be expressed in terms of the gleaming whiteness of clothes, hair, beard and throne (Daniel 7:9–10). Israel thought of this dazzling presence of God as being withdrawn when the Temple was destroyed (*I-Kabhod*, 'the Glory has departed') and hoped for the end of all things as a time when the light of God's presence would be restored:

Arise, shine out, Jerusalem,
for your light has come,
the Glory of the Lord is rising upon you,
though night still covers the earth
and darkness the peoples.
Above you the Lord now rises
and above you his Glory appears.
The nations come to your light
and kings to your dawning brightness (Isaiah 60:1–3).

What is therefore being claimed for Jesus in this section of

John's gospel is something far more breathtaking than that he is the fulfilment of a number of messianic texts. If he is the Light of the World, then he is the *Kabhod*, the manifestation of God among men, the making visible in our world of the God who by definition cannot be seen. He does not merely mediate the light which is God: he is the reflection, the untarnished mirror of that light on earth. He is the Light of the World because through him the light of God is radiated to the world and communicated to men. 'Light of the World' is a title more explicitly divine than any other in the gospel.

JUDGMENT

The theme of light is closely connected with that of judgment and discrimination. It is of the nature of light to show things up for what they are, to penetrate through make-believe to the reality behind it. A neon light is far more discriminating – and cruel as many will agree – than candlelight.

The coming of the light necessarily divides people into two camps: the sons of light who welcome it, and the sons of darkness who run from it. Christ's coming is the coming of light. His is not the gentle, beneficent glow of Holman Hunt's candle-stump. His is the fiery brilliance which forces men to declare themselves for or against. The gospel pages are full of this note of crisis and urgency. Jesus does not need to pronounce judgment or condemnation: men judge themselves by the way they react. You show which side you are on as soon as the light appears.

People will in fact, says John, turn their backs on the light when it comes. They will do more: they will find the light so unbearable that they will try to put it out. But the outcome is inevitable. Light cannot be put out by the darkness; it will always be the winner. Strike a match anywhere in the darkness and the darkness is gone; it cannot hold its own. The theme is celebrated in the bible's opening lines, where the primeval darkness is vanquished by the simple decree, 'Let there be light.'

So the attempt to blot out the light is doomed to failure. The more determined the attempt, the more strongly the light shines. And the more surely the sons of darkness condemn themselves.

WHO IS JESUS?

It is against this background of the feast of Tabernacles, the themes of water, light, glory and judgment, and the hopes for the messianic age, that John places the following discourse to provide a frame for his story of the man born blind:

As the Jewish feast of Tabernacles drew near, Jesus' brothers said to him, 'Why not leave this place and go to Judaea?' ... Jesus answered, 'The right time for me has not come yet' ... However, after his brothers had left for the festival, he went up as well ... When the festival was half over, Jesus went to the Temple and began to teach ... He said:

'Do not keep judging according to appearances;
let your judgment be according to what is right ...
There is one who sent me and I really come from him,
and you do not know him, but I know him
because I have come from him and it was he who sent me.'

They would have arrested him then, but because his hour had not yet come no one laid a hand upon him ... Then Jesus said:

I shall remain with you for only a short time now;
then I shall go back to the one who sent me.'

On the last day of the festival, the Great Day, Jesus stood there and cried out:

'If any man is thirsty, let him come to me!
Let the man come and drink who believes in me!'

As scripture says: From his breast shall flow fountains of living water. He was speaking of the Spirit which those who believed in him were to receive; for the Spirit had not yet been given because Jesus had not yet been glorified . . .

Nicodemus said, 'Surely the Law does not allow us to pass judgment on a man without giving him a hearing and discovering what he is about . . .

At daybreak Jesus appeared in the Temple again; and as all the people came to him, he sat down and began to teach them . . . He said:

'I am the light of the world;
anyone who follows me will not be walking in the dark;
he will have the light of life' . . .

At this the Pharisees said to him, 'You are testifying on your own behalf; your testimony is not valid'. Jesus replied:

'It is true that I am testifying on my own behalf,
but my testimony is still valid,
because I know
where I came from and where I am going;
but you do not know
where I come from or where I am going.
You judge by human standards;
I judge no one,
but if I judge,
my judgment will be sound' . . .

They asked him, 'Where is your Father?' Jesus answered:

'You do not know me, nor do you know my Father;
if you did know me, you would know my Father as well.'

He spoke these words . . . in the Temple. No one arrested him, because his hour had not yet come. Again he said to them: . . .

'If you do not believe what I am
you will die in your sins . . .
When you have lifted up the Son of Man,
then you will know what I am . . .
If I speak the truth, why do you not believe me?
A child of God listens to the words of God;
if you refuse to listen,
it is because you are not God's children . . .
If I were to seek my own glory
that would be no glory at all;
my glory is conferred by the Father,
by the one of whom you say, "He is our God"
although you do not know him . . .
But I know him, and I faithfully keep his word.
Your father Abraham rejoiced
to think that he would see my Day;
he saw it and was glad.'

The Jews then said, 'You are not fifty yet, and you have seen
Abraham!' Jesus replied:

'I tell you most solemnly,
before Abraham ever was,
I Am.'

At this they picked up stones to throw at him; but Jesus hid
himself and left the Temple . . . Jesus said:

'As long as the day lasts
I must carry out the work of the one who sent me;
the night will soon be here when no one can work.
As long as I am in the world
I am the light of the world . . .
It is for judgment
that I have come into this world,
so that those without sight may see
and those with sight turn blind . . .
The sheep follow the shepherd
because they know his voice.

They never follow a stranger
but run away from him:
they do not recognize the voice of strangers . . .
The thief comes
only to steal and kill and destroy.
I have come
so that they may have life
and have it to the full . . .
I am the good shepherd:
I know my own
and my own know me,
just as the Father knows me
and I know the Father . . .
The sheep that belong to me listen to my voice;
I know them and they follow me.
I give them eternal life;
they will never be lost
and no one will ever steal them from me.
The Father who gave them to me is greater than
    anyone,
and no one can steal from the Father.
The Father and I are one.'

The Jews fetched stones to stone him, so Jesus said to them, 'I
have done many good works for you to see, works from my
Father; for which of these are you stoning me?' The Jews
answered him, 'We are not stoning you for doing a good work
but for blasphemy: you are only a man and you claim to be
God.' Jesus answered: . . .

'If I am not doing my Father's work,
there is no need to believe me;
but if I am doing it,
then even if you refuse to believe in me,
at least believe in the work I do;
then you will know for sure
that the Father is in me and I am in the Father.'

They wanted to arrest him then, but he eluded them. He

went back again to the far side of the Jordan to stay in the district where John had once been baptising (John 7:2–10:39).

Only excerpts from this section of John's gospel have been quoted here. They should be sufficient to show how the whole four chapters are held together by the themes opened out above.

The theme of light provides the basic pattern. Light is self-authenticating. Other things need light to be recognized for what they are, but what can throw light on light itself? In the same way, truth is its own witness. It is recognized automatically, as like is recognized by like. Anyone who does not recognize the truth when it is presented to him condemns himself. Anyone who turns his back on the light consigns himself to darkness.

Who is this who can force men to make such a fateful decision? The question is being asked throughout these chapters, and the argument goes to and fro.

He is one who is of God. He comes from God. Like the waters of Siloam, he is one who has been 'sent'. He is one who claims to be equal to God. He is one to whom John must eventually give the divine title 'I Am'.

And this divinity of his ('What I am') will be seen most clearly when he dies. The section is filled with repeated references to the efforts to arrest him, to the attempts to stone him, to his inevitable death, to his 'Hour', to the lifting up of the Son of Man on the cross.

Why this link between his divinity and his death? Because the attempt to blot out the light is doomed to failure. Light will always win. Indeed, the more darkness there is, the brighter the light shines out: stars are only at their best against a black sky. And so Jesus' death, in one sense the hour of darkness, is by no means his extinction. It is his most brilliant manifestation. This is the moment when he is glorified, when the waters of the divine Spirit flow from his breast. When he dies on the cross he is most fully the light, revealing most clearly the light that God is, and so bringing enlightenment to eyes that were blind.

Let us finally listen to the miracle story itself, which puts this profound theology into a concrete form. What a loss it would have been had John left all his theologizing in the abstract, and not expressed it from time to time in concrete stories which people can tell each other down the ages:

As Jesus went along, he saw a man who had been blind from birth. His disciples asked him, 'Rabbi, who sinned, this man or his parents, for him to have been born blind?' 'Neither he nor his parents sinned,' Jesus answered 'he was born blind so that the works of God might be displayed in him . . .' Having said this, he spat on the ground, made clay with the spittle, put this over the eyes of the blind man, and said to him, 'Go and wash in the Pool of Siloam' (a name that means 'sent'). So the blind man went off and washed himself, and came away with his sight restored.

His neighbours and people who earlier had seen him begging said, 'Isn't this the man who used to sit and beg?' Some said, 'Yes, it is the same one'. Others said, 'No, he only looks like him.' The man himself said, 'I am the man.' So they said to him, 'Then how do your eyes come to be open?' 'The man called Jesus' he answered 'made clay, daubed my eyes with it and said to me, "Go and wash at Siloam"; so I went, and when I washed I could see.' They asked, 'Where is he?' I don't know' he answered.

They brought the man who had been blind to the Pharisees. It had been a sabbath day when Jesus made the clay and opened the man's eyes, so when the Pharisees asked him how he had come to see, he said, 'He put clay on my eyes, and I washed, and I can see.' Then some of the Pharisees said, 'This man cannot be from God: he does not keep the sabbath.' Others said, 'How could a sinner produce signs like this?' And there was disagreement among them. So they spoke to the blind man again, 'What have you to say about him yourself, now that he has opened your eyes?' 'He is a prophet' replied the man.

However, the Jews would not believe that the man had been blind and had gained his sight, without first sending for his parents and asking them, 'Is this man really your son who you say was born blind? If so, how is it that he is now able to see? His parents answered, 'We know he is our son and we know he was born blind, but we don't know how it is that he can see now, or who opened his eyes. He is old enough: let him speak for himself.' His parents spoke like this out of fear of the Jews, who had already agreed to expel from the synagogue anyone who should acknowledge Jesus as the Christ. This was why his parents said, 'He is old enough; ask him.'

So the Jews again sent for the man and said to him, 'Give glory to God! For our part, we know that this man is a sinner.' The man answered, 'I don't know if he is a sinner; I only know that I was blind and now I can see.' They said to him, 'What did he do to you? How did he open your eyes?' He replied, 'I have told you once and you wouldn't listen. Why do you want to hear it all again? Do you want to become his disciples too?' At this they hurled abuse at him: 'You can be his disciple,' they said 'we are disciples of Moses: we know that God spoke to Moses, but as for this man, we don't know where he comes from.' The man replied, 'Now here is an astonishing thing! He has opened my eyes and you don't know where he comes from! We know that God doesn't listen to sinners, but God does listen to men who are devout and do his will. Ever since the world began it is unheard of for anyone to open the eyes of a man who was born blind; if this man were not from God, he couldn't do a thing.' 'Are you trying to teach us,' they replied 'and you a sinner through and through, since you were born!' And they drove him away.

Jesus heard that they had driven him away, and when he found him he said to him, 'Do you believe in the Son of Man?' 'Sir,' the man replied 'tell me who he is that I may believe in him.' Jesus said, 'You are looking at him; he is speaking to you.' The man said, 'Lord, I believe,' and worshipped him (John 9:1–38).

79

The background provided above should have made it possible for the story to stand out in its full dimensions.

Anyone who wants to see it simply as a record of a remarkable cure worked by Jesus many centuries ago is entitled to do so. But in the context of John's gospel the story is something far more serious. It is a statement about the whole of mankind and its relationship to the crucified and risen Christ.

John is saying that all men are born in the dark. They come out of this darkness when they are washed in the Water or breathe the Spirit of the one 'sent' from God. That is when the original darkness passes away and a new creation arises out of the clay.

But this Water, this Spirit, is not available until Jesus is glorified through his death and resurrection. It is only then that he becomes the divine light bringing sight to the blind, because it is only then that he fully reveals God, as self-sharing light. Only when the Son of man is lifted up will men know that he is the 'I Am'.

So Easter day is like Judgment day. From Easter onward, the light shows men up for what they are; they will either run away from it and remain in darkness, or welcome it and share its glory.

The story, then, for one who has seen the risen Jesus, is, like all the gospel stories, a resurrection story. Its meaning is summed up in its key phrases: *As Jesus passes by, he sees a man who has been blind from birth. Jesus says to him, 'I am the Light of the World', and tells him to wash in the Water 'sent' from above. Then he says, 'Do you believe in the Son of Man?' The man asks, 'Who is he?' Jesus replies, 'You are now seeing him for the first time; he is now speaking to you.'*

ENLIGHTENMENT

We have seen above how John's stories tend to have a sacramental dimension. this is not to say that they are simply allegories of the Christian sacraments: their reference is always much wider. Their message is addressed to all men, even though they do not know the sacraments. But for the Christian reader, already living a sacramental life, the miracle stories are an assurance that the reality of which they speak comes to him in the sacraments.

In this instance, the pool of water in which the blind man washes reminds the Christian reader of the waters of baptism. Certainly the early Fathers spoke of baptism as the *phōtismos* or enlightenment of man, and they took this usage from the New Testament:

> As for those people who were once brought into the light, and tasted the gift from heaven, and received a share of the Holy Spirit, and appreciated the good message of God and the powers of the world to come and yet in spite of this have fallen away – it is impossible for them to be renewed a second time (Hebrews 6:4–6).

> Remember all the sufferings that you had to meet after you received enlightenment, in earlier days; sometimes by being yourselves publicly exposed to insults and violence, and sometimes as associates of others who were treated in the same way. For you not only shared in the sufferings of those who were in prison, but you happily accepted being stripped of your belongings, knowing that you owned something that was better and lasting. Be as confident now, then, since the reward is so great (Hebrews 10:32–5).

At its deepest level, the story reminds the Christian that, enlightened by baptism, he is called upon like the blind man to profess Christ openly before men, even at the cost of persecution. The presence of the man of insight is always going to be an embarrassment to the unenlightened. Jesus himself was excommunicated, which only proved his point: there is not and cannot be any communion between light and darkness.

81

8. New Life to the Dead

(*John* 11)

Chapter 11 is one of the most important pages in John's gospel. This would be obvious even on a count of words: if the first two chapters are counted as an introduction and one begins with the body of the gospel at chapter 3, then there are exactly as many pages of the gospel after chapter 11 as before it. But it is central in a much more serious sense, in the whole design of the gospel (see the plan on p. 125).

It has been explained above on p. 39 that the prologue of this gospel (1:1–18) announces the three principal themes with which the gospel is concerned: Jesus as the Life, the Light and the Glory of God. The first theme of Life begins in chapter 3 with Nicodemus coming to hear Jesus, and ends in chapter 7 with Nicodemus pleading that Jesus be given a hearing:

> Nicodemus – the same man who had come to Jesus earlier – said to them, 'Surely the Law does not allow us to pass judgment on a man without giving him a hearing?' (7:50–1).

The second theme of Light covers chapters 8–10, and finishes with Jesus returning to the place where his ministry first began in the introductory chapters:

> Jesus went back again to the far side of the Jordan to stay in the district where John had once been baptising (10:40).

This double use of *inclusio* gives the reader the feeling that those first two themes are well and truly completed, the knots having been neatly tied both inside (from chapter 3 to chapter 7) and outside (from chapter 1 to chapter 10).

By the end of chapter 10, therefore, one is ready to begin

reading the account of Jesus' passion and death, which announces the third theme of Glory in its opening lines:

Now the hour has come
for the Son of Man to be glorified.

And indeed everything that has been written in the earlier chapters has prepared the reader for this, from the opening story's statement, 'Woman, my hour has not come yet' (2:4). These words are repeated again and again in the mounting opposition described in chapters 7 to 10. By the end of chapter 10 we are prepared for the passion of Jesus.

The account of the passion begins in chapter 12. Chapter 11 stands between, as a bridge linking the first two themes with the third. John is taking a last look back at the themes of Life and Light which he has developed over the preceding chapters, to draw the threads together for the last time, in order to show us how Jesus, the Life and Light of God, becomes the Glory of God. There is no chapter in the gospel which is more detailed, no page more pregnant with meaning.

WHAT KIND OF STORY?

Before we read it, we would do well to ask ourselves what kind of story we are expecting. When we read what is apparently a record of a man dying, lying dead four days and then being called back to life again, what sort of reality do we think it is meant to convey?

Without prejudging the issue, it would be dishonest not to draw attention to two other texts which bear a striking resemblance to this story. Our story states, without further introduction: 'There was a man named Lazarus . . . and he died . . . and he rose from the dead.' Luke's gospel has a story which states, again without any introduction:

There was a rich man . . . and at his gate there lay a poor man named Lazarus . . . and he died . . . and the rich man said, 'Send him to my brothers . . . If someone comes to them from the dead, they will repent.' Then Abraham said to him, 'If they will not listen either to Moses or to the prophets, they will not be convinced even if someone should rise from the dead' (Luke 16:19–31).

This story we call a parable. Why? What should we call John's story?

Again, John's story concludes with the words: 'Jesus cried in a loud voice, "Lazarus, come out!" And the dead man came out of the tomb.' Yet six chapters earlier John had already recorded the words:

As the Father raises the dead and gives them life
so the Son gives life to anyone he chooses;
for the Father judges no one;
he has entrusted all judgment to the Son . . .
Whoever listens to my words,
and believes in the one who sent me,
has eternal life;
without being brought to judgment
he has passed from death to life.
I tell you most solemnly,
the hour will come – in fact it is here already –
when the dead will hear the voice of the Son of God,
and all who hear it will live . . .
The hour is coming
when the dead will leave their graves
at the sound of his voice (John 5:21–8).

This extract we call a discourse of Jesus. What should we call the extract from chapter 11? The least one can say is that it is clearly intended to illustrate the same truth.

THE STORY

There was a man named Lazarus who lived in the village of Bethany with the two sisters, Mary and Martha, and he was ill . . . The sisters sent this message to Jesus, 'Lord the man you love is ill.' On receiving the message, Jesus said, 'This sickness will end, not in death but in God's glory, and through it the Son of God will be glorified.'

Jesus loved Martha and her sister and Lazarus, yet when he heard that Lazarus was ill he stayed where he was for two more days before saying to the disciples, 'Let us go to Judaea.' The disciples said, 'Rabbi, it is not long since the Jews wanted to stone you; are you going back again?' Jesus replied:

'Are there not twelve hours in the day?
A man can walk in the daytime without stumbling
because he has the light of this world to see by;
but if he walks at night he stumbles,
because there is no light to guide him.'

He said that and then added, 'Our friend Lazarus is resting, I am going to wake him.' The disciples said to him, 'Lord, if he is able to rest he is sure to get better.' The phrase Jesus used referred to the death of Lazarus, but they thought that by 'rest' he meant 'sleep', so Jesus put it plainly, 'Lazarus is dead; and for your sake I am glad I was not there because now you will believe. But let us go to him.' Then Thomas – known as the Twin – said to the other disciples, 'Let us go too, and die with him.'

On arriving, Jesus found that Lazarus had been in the tomb for four days already. Bethany is only about two miles from Jerusalem, and many Jews had come to Martha and Mary to sympathize with them over their brother. When Martha heard that Jesus had come she went to meet him. Mary remained sitting in the house. Martha said to Jesus, 'If you had been here, my brother would not have died, but I know that, even now, whatever you ask of God, he will grant you.' 'Your brother' said Jesus to her 'will rise again.' Martha said, 'I know he will rise again at the resurrection on the last day.' Jesus said:

'I am the resurrection.
If anyone believes in me,

even though he dies he will live,
and whoever lives and believes in me
will never die.
Do you believe this?'

'Yes, Lord,' she said 'I believe you are the Christ, the Son of God, the one who was to come into this world.'

When she had said this, she went and called her sister Mary, saying in a low voice, 'The Master is here and wants to see you.' Hearing this, Mary got up quickly and went to him. Jesus had not yet come into the village; he was still at the place where Martha had met him. When the Jews who were in the house sympathizing with Mary saw her get up so quickly and go out, they followed her, thinking that she was going to the tomb to weep there.

Mary went to Jesus, and as soon as she saw him she threw herself at his feet, saying, 'Lord, if you had been here, my brother would not have died.' At the sight of her tears, and those of the Jews who followed her, Jesus said in great distress, with a sigh that came straight from the heart, 'Where have you put him?' They said, 'Lord, come and see.' Jesus wept; and the Jews said, 'See how much he loved him!' But there were some who remarked, 'He opened the eyes of the blind man, could he not have prevented this man's death?' Still sighing, Jesus reached the tomb; it was a cave with a stone to close the opening. Jesus said, 'Take the stone away.' Martha said to him, 'Lord, by now he will smell; this is the fourth day.' Jesus replied, 'Have I not told you that if you believe you will see the glory of God?' So they took away the stone. Then Jesus lifted up his eyes and said:

'Father, I thank you for hearing my prayer.
I knew indeed that you always hear me,
but I speak
for the sake of all these who stand round me,
so that they may believe it was you who sent me.'

When he had said this, he cried in a loud voice, 'Lazarus, here! Come out!' The dead man came out, his feet and hands bound with bands of stuff and a cloth round his face. Jesus said to them, 'Unbind him, let him go free.'

Many of the Jews who had come to visit Mary and had seen what he did believed in him, but some of them went to tell the Pharisees what Jesus had done. Then the chief priests and Pharisees called a meeting. 'Here is this man working all these signs' they said 'and what action are we taking? If we let him go on in this way everybody will believe in him, and the Romans will come and destroy the Holy Place and our nation.' One of them, Caiaphas, the high priest that year, said, 'You don't seem to have grasped the situation at all; you fail to see that it is better for one man to die for the people, than for the whole nation to be destroyed.' He did not speak in his own person, it was as high priest that he made this prophecy that Jesus was to die for the nation – and not for the nation only, but to gather together in unity the scattered children of God. From that day they were determined to kill him. So Jesus no longer went about openly among the Jews, but left the district for a town called Ephraim, in the country bordering on the desert, and stayed there with his disciples.

The Jewish Passover drew near (John 11:1–55).

LOOKING FOR CLUES

Many of the clues to the meaning of this story will be becoming familiar to those who have followed the argument so far. They have already been used in one or other of the previous miracle stories to indicate what significance these stories had for John.

Our story begins with a reference to the glory of God and of Jesus:

This sickness will end, not in death but in God's glory, and through it the Son of God will be glorified.

I have already pointed out that in Greek the word 'glory' means more than it does in English. It is not an invitation to give three cheers for God and a big round of applause for Jesus. It is a technical word for the very reality of God as made visible to men. In some sense, the word cannot be applied to the Jesus who walks the lanes of Palestine; throughout the gospel John insists that it really only fits him at Calvary. It is the death of Jesus which is the glorification of Jesus and the glorification of God. 'What God is' will become manifest and accessible to men only when the body of Jesus is glorified through death. By using the word in this chapter, John indicates that he sees the story of Lazarus as another preview of Jesus' own death and resurrection. He repeats the point with some emphasis as the story comes to its climax:

> Have I not told you that if you believe
> you will see the glory of God?

Next, when Jesus is questioned about the wisdom of venturing into Judaea again, he replies in words that recall the theme of the preceding chapters:

> A man can walk in the daytime without stumbling
> because he has the light of this world to see by;
> but if he walks at night he stumbles,
> because there is no light to guide him.

In themselves, the words might be no more than a common proverb: Jesus must make use of the time and opportunities available to him. But in the context of the preceding pages, where Jesus himself is the Light of this world, the words contain more than a hint of the attempt to blot him out. The Judaeans must be given a chance to see this Light while it still shines. Our story is to be read as another illustration of the impotence of darkness in the face of light, and as another reference to Jesus' own death and resurrection.

When Martha declares her faith in Jesus as 'the one who is to come' she is using, as was explained above, an official title for the messiah, the culmination of Old Testament expectations. It is a weak enough word to use in a context where Jesus is being called the very Glory of God. But it is interesting that the recognition of Jesus as the fulfilment of Israel's hopes is linked with this meditation on his death and resurrection. He does not show himself first as messiah and then add his death and resurrection as a kind of bonus. Nor is his death a regrettable interruption in his messianic plans. His death is the very substance of which his messiah-ship is made. For John, Jesus does not really fulfil his messianic task, he is not really 'the one who is to come', except in the context of his dying and rising.

The story concludes with the statement: 'From that day they were determined to kill him.' This too repeats a theme of the previous chapters. Whatever the reality behind this story of the death of Lazarus, it is somehow inextricably tied up with the death of Jesus himself; the one necessarily involves the other. All the controversies in the preceding pages, the growing opposition, the attempts to arrest him, the threats to stone him – these come to a climax in this verse. Here his death-knell is sounded. Whatever else the story of Lazarus is about, it is certainly about Jesus' condemnation to death. That is why the very last words of the story are highly significant: 'The Jewish Passover drew near.' The hour has come for Jesus to make the journey whereby he passes over from this world to the Father.

For anyone who already knows the story of Jesus' death – as John does and as the reader is presumed to – there are a whole number of minor details in the story of Lazarus which cannot help reminding him of it. Mary at Jesus' feet, weeping her heart out over her brother, is a preview of the scene in which it is Jesus' death she will lament. Jesus' words to her, 'Where have you put him (Lazarus)?' forestall the words she will then use, 'Tell me where you have put him (Jesus).' The tears of Jesus and his cry of distress over the death of Lazarus are a premonition of the anguish and agony he will suffer a week later in the face of his own death. The tomb with a stone to close the opening, the bandages and the face cloth – these too are clearly anticipations of the last chapters in the gospel.

These apparently deliberate echoes suggest that a clue should be found in the threefold repetition of the hopelessness of the situation. This is emphasized with almost brutal reality:

'Lazarus had been in the tomb for four days already', 'If you had been here my brother would not have died', 'By now he will smell; this is the fourth day.' I have pointed out a number of times above that this is a favourite theme of John: the uselessness of water for a wedding party and the desperate situation of the cripple at the pool; the inadequacy of five loaves for thousands of hungry people and the congenital blindness of the Jerusalem beggar, who needed not merely a cure but a whole new creation. This is all that the human situation can provide, just as at Calvary the only thing that could be physically seen was a dead body. Out of that humanly hopeless situation faith has to make something, and will do so. 'Have I not told you that if you believe you will see the glory of God?'

THE HUMAN CONDITION

The hopelessness of the human situation is underlined in the word used to describe Lazarus' condition. In the opening line he is said to be *asthenēs*, and later it is stated that 'this *astheneia* will end in God's glory.' In the context of the story, of course, the word means 'sick, ill', and so it is always translated. But the literal meaning is actually wider. *Astheneia* means 'weakness', and the New Testament uses the word frequently to express the poverty and helplessness of the human condition, especially of Jesus himself.

Everyone is familiar with the words of Jesus in Gethsemane, 'The spirit is willing but the flesh is *weak*', and the description applies first of all to him, who became flesh. The epistle to the Hebrews uses the same words when it comes to speak of Jesus' agony in the face of death:

It is not as if we had a high priest who was incapable of feeling our *weaknesses* with us; but we have one who has been tempted in every way that we are . . . and so he can sympathize with those who are ignorant or uncertain because he too lives in the limitations of *weakness* . . . He offered up prayer and entreaty, aloud and in silent tears, to the one who had the power to save him out of death, and he submitted so humbly that his prayer was heard. Although he was Son, he learnt to obey through suffering (Hebrews 4:15–5:8).

And Paul finds he needs the same word to describe not only the suffering death of Jesus, but the whole Christian message about Jesus' death:

The language of the cross may be illogical to those who are not on the way to salvation, but those of us who are on the way see it as God's power to save . . . God wanted to save those who have faith through the foolishness of the message that we preach. And so, while the Jews demand miracles and the Greeks look for wisdom, here are we preaching a crucified Christ . . . For God's foolishness is wiser than human wisdom, and God's *weakness* is stronger than human strength . . . It was to shame the wise that God chose what is foolish by human reckoning, and to shame what is strong that he chose what is *weak* by human reckoning (1 Corinthians 1:18–27).

At the end of the same epistle, where he deals explicitly with the resurrection, it is still the same word that he uses:

The thing that is sown is perishable
but what is raised is imperishable;
the thing that is sown is contemptible
but what is raised is glorious;
the thing that is sown is *weak*
but what is raised is powerful;
when it is sown it embodies the soul,
when it is raised it embodies the Spirit (1 Corinthians
    15:42–4).

So that eventually, in his second letter to Corinth, he can even speak of the power of that resurrection in himself in the same terms:

You want proof, you say, that it is Christ speaking in me: you have known him not as a *weakling*, but as a power among you? Yes, but he was crucified through *weakness*, and still he lives now through the power of God. So then, we are *weak*, as he was, but we shall live with him, through the power of God, for your benefit (2 Corinthians 13:3–4).

No one would pretend that any of these texts were in John's mind when he spoke of Lazarus' *weakness*. He is not quoting Paul. But both he and Paul have their eyes fixed on the same mystery.

THE MEANING

What, then, is the story about? Whatever may be said of the death of Lazarus, for the Christian the story is certainly intended to evoke the death of Jesus. The repeated threats against Jesus' life, the forebodings about his future and the dangers he is running, the approach of the last Passover, the decision to kill him, the reference to the Light being snuffed out, the dozen reminiscences of the scene at Calvary – these make it clear beyond doubt that John is using the story of Lazarus' death as a symbol of what is for him far more important, the death of Jesus.

But if the death of Jesus, then also his resurrection, because John will not have us think of one without the other. If the telling of Lazarus' death is meant to make the reader think of the death of Jesus, then certainly the story of Lazarus' raising is meant to remind him of the raising of Jesus. Lazarus' illness, the weakness of the human condition which Jesus shares with all men, 'will end, *not* in death but in God's glory'. Its ultimate purpose is not the dead end of death, but a life-giving manifestation of what God is really like. The Glory is achieved, not in spite of death but through it. It is in the decomposing figure of the story, emphasized with shocking reality, that the reality of God is clearest to those with eyes to see. In the story, Lazarus dies, and for the sake of his disciples

Jesus declares that he is *glad* that things have gone to that extremity, so that they may be forced to exercise their faith (verse 15), and not keep on searching for things which will make faith unnecessary.

In short, because of the death of Jesus, death can no longer be thought of as a cul-de-sac. It is a pass-over, whereby humanity achieves the perfection for which it was created: union with God. That is why the actual physical event of dying loses its importance. One sentence in the story says so explicitly: 'Our friend is only resting, I am going to wake him.' But then the whole story has really been saying the same thing: dying in union with a Christ of such life-giving power holds no more terrors.

OUR RESURRECTION

The key to the whole story, therefore, lies in Jesus' statement: 'I am the resurrection.' By revealing to us, in his own death, what God is like, Jesus has become *our* resurrection. We are not to think, as the Martha of the story does, that the reality of God is somehow remote from us, something we put our faith in, but which is in another world running parallel to ours and never really meeting until the end. Jesus' contemporaries thought this way, and many Christians continue to do so. 'My meeting with God' they tend to say 'will come on the last day. My resurrection into the fullness of God's life is still a long way off. I have my death to worry about first; I'll think about my resurrection later.'

It is to such people that Jesus says, 'I *am* the resurrection.' He is the superabundant life of God made available to us here and now. The divine life has been embodied in a man like ourselves. This means that he is the resurrection of the body, infusing into mankind a life against which death cannot hold out.

Three times the story insists that this cannot be appreciated without faith:

I am glad Lazarus is dead, because now you will believe.

93

If you will believe you will see the glory of God.

I speak so that they may believe it was you who sent me.

The previous miracle stories have all placed the same emphasis on faith. What the stories have been about cannot be proved, only personally experienced through faith. It is in the commitment of faith that the resurrection becomes a reality for us. The moment when we pass from death to life is no longer on the last day, or even on our deathbed, but when we 'hear the voice of the Son of God and believe'. The person who accepts Jesus as the revelation and the gift of God never really dies, never really loses that one life which really matters, which is to know God as he is, through the Son.

The deepest meaning of the story, therefore, is not that Jesus has rather more powerful magic than other wonder workers. It is that through his death and resurrection Jesus is the one source of eternal life. It can be summed up, like the other miracle stories, in its key phrases: *Jesus was given the message, 'Lord, he whom you love is weak.' Jesus said, 'This weakness will end, not in death but in the manifestation of God's glory.' Then he stayed where he was for two more days. Mary was told, 'The Master is here, and he is calling you.' And Jesus said, 'I am the resurrection. If anyone believes in me, even though he dies he lives on. Do you believe this?' 'Yes, Lord, I believe that you are the Christ, the Son of God, the one who is to come.'*

9. Saved from Drowning

(*John* 21)

John's gospel ends in chapter 20 with the famous saying:

> There were many other signs that Jesus worked and the
> disciples saw, but they are not recorded in this book. These
> are recorded to nourish and sustain your faith in Jesus as the
> Christ, the Son of God, so that through your faith you may
> have life.

This is so clearly a signing-off line that everyone has always
recognized the chapter that follows as an appendix, written
either by John himself as a postscript, or by his disciples and
editors. This latter is in fact more likely; John himself seems to
have restricted his resurrection stories to Jerusalem, and
chapter 21 takes us into Galilee. But it contains an interesting
miracle story which has much in common with those we have
considered above. A short analysis of this story is therefore
appropriate, before coming to a conclusion.

WHO MOVED THE STORY

One of the remarkable things about this story is that although
it is the first to tell of a miracle performed explicitly by the
risen Christ, it is scarcely distinguishable from the story of the
earthly Jesus recounted on the opening pages of Luke's gospel.
There too we read of a miraculous draught of fish, and a call to
Peter and his companions to follow Jesus, with the suggestion
that from now onwards it is men they are going to catch (see
Luke 5: 1–11 and parallels). Who moved the story? Did Luke
transfer what was originally a story about the resurrection into
his account of Jesus' public life? Or did John's gospel transfer
what was originally a story from Jesus' ministry into the
resurrection narrative, in order to suggest that the following of
Christ in its fullest sense was not possible until after the

resurrection? Whoever did the moving, it is interesting that he felt free to do so. From whichever side of Jesus' death the story originated, it is for the evangelist always a resurrection story, in which what is primary is not what Jesus did in the past, but what he does now because he is risen from the dead and lives on into the present.

Jesus showed himself again to the disciples. It was by the Sea of Tiberias, and it happened like this: Simon Peter, Thomas called the Twin, Nathanael from Cana in Galilee, the sons of Zebedee and two more of his disciples were together. Simon Peter said, 'I'm going fishing.' They replied, 'We'll come with you.' They went out and got into the boat but caught nothing that night.

It was light by now and there stood Jesus on the shore, though the disciples did not realize that it was Jesus, Jesus called out, 'Have you caught anything, friends?' And when they answered, 'No', he said, 'Throw the net out to starboard and you'll find something.' So they dropped the net, and there were so many fish that they could not haul it in. The disciple Jesus loved said to Peter, 'It is the Lord.' At these words 'It is the Lord', Simon Peter, who had practically nothing on, wrapped his cloak round him and jumped into the water. The other disciples came on in the boat, towing the net and the fish; they were only about a hundred yards from land.

As soon as they came ashore they saw that there was some bread there, and a charcoal fire with fish cooking on it. Jesus said, 'Bring some of the fish you have just caught.' Simon Peter went aboard and dragged the net to the shore, full of big fish, one hundred and fifty-three of them; and in spite of there being so many the net was not broken. Jesus said to them, 'Come and have breakfast.' None of the disciples was bold enough to ask, 'Who are you?'; they knew quite well it was the Lord. Jesus then stepped forward, took the bread and gave it to them, and the same with the fish . . .

After the meal Jesus said to Simon Peter, 'Simon son of John, do you love me more than these others do?' He answered, 'Yes Lord, you know I love you.' Jesus said to him, 'Feed my lambs.' A second time he said to him, 'Simon son of John, do you love me?' He replied, 'Yes Lord, you know I love you.' Jesus said to him, 'Look after my sheep.' Then he said to him a third time, 'Simon son of John, do you love me?' Peter was upset that he asked him the third time, 'Do you love me?' and said, 'Lord, you know everything; you know I love you.' Jesus said to him, 'Feed my sheep.

> 'I tell you most solemnly,
> when you were young
> you put on your own belt
> and walked where you liked;
> but when you grow old
> you will stretch out your hands,
> and somebody else will put a belt round you
> and take you where you would rather not go.'

In these words he indicated the kind of death by which Peter would give glory to God. After this he said, 'Follow me' (John 21:1–19).

LOOKING FOR CLUES

The story points the contrast between the unlikely material to hand and the superabundance of the outcome. The disciples had nothing to show for their night's fishing, and yet at Jesus' command the haul is so enormous they cannot handle it. The theme occurs so frequently in this gospel that it would seem to be referred to here too. In the last analysis the superabundance is to be verified in the risen Christ, full of grace and truth (1:14), who came so that men may have life to the full (10:10), and of that fullness all who believe in him have received (1:16), to the extent that they will never hunger or thirst again (4:14).

The story connects the miracle particularly with two disciples, Simon Peter and 'the disciple whom Jesus loved'. It may be significant that the same two are linked in the story of the visit to the tomb in the previous chapter, where their reactions are much the same as here. There, the unnamed disciple is the first to reach the empty tomb, but does not enter; it is Peter who is the first to go in (20:3–10). Here also, the unnamed disciple is the first to see the implications of what has happened and cries out, 'It is the Lord'; but it is Peter who jumps – if not to a conclusion certainly into the heaving sea. The story echoes other references to Peter's boat and his foundational part in the formation of the Easter faith of the first disciples (see chapter 6 above).

The count of fish given in the story may be significant. Greek naturalists of the day made their own count of the different species of fish they knew, and arrived at the number hundred and fifty-three. This may be a real figure, but it is equally possible that it is symbolic since it is the sum of all the numbers from one to seventeen (itself the addition of the 'perfect' numbers ten and seven). If there is any reference here to that Greek number – and it is only a possibility, not a certainty – then the text could be suggesting the universality of the apostles' mission. After all, Matthew's gospel ends on the same note: the risen Christ commissions the eleven to 'go and make disciples of all nations' (Matthew 28:19). It is only in the light of the resurrection that the apostles saw their mission as spreading beyond Judaism, where Jesus' own ministry had been confined, to the ends of the earth.

A final clue to the meaning of the story is to be found in the emphasis on love in the closing scene between Jesus and Peter. In John's gospel this is most significant. In this book I have limited myself to a study of the miracle stories, and so have not analysed the farewell discourses of Jesus contained in chapters 14 to 17. But those chapters make it clear that, for John, love is precisely the Glory of God, that is to say, the manifestation of what God really is. And Jesus' death is his entry into that Glory, his 'glorification' of God, because of all the moments in his life this revealed God most clearly. That God really *is* love, not something else, is seen most vividly in Jesus' acceptance of his death. And if the mystery of Christ is ultimately intelligible only in terms of love, the same must be true of the Christian. Especially of Peter. If he is to lead and feed the flock of Christ, he cannot do so in any other way than that used by Jesus, which is love. If he is to follow in the footsteps of Jesus, to share the

Glory which Jesus entered, he must be willing to lay down his life, confident that out of this death too God can and will bring life:

> In these words he indicated the kind of death (martyrdom) by which Peter would glorify God. After this he said, 'Follow me.'

THE MEANING

What, then, has the story been about? Anyone who wishes to read it as a reporter's account of a prodigy that took place on the Galilee lakeside, and of the conversation which followed, must feel free to do so. I am suggesting that the story is told for another and deeper purpose. Whatever the story may rest on historically, it is primarily about the mystery of the risen Christ. It is about the unexpected transformation of failure into success, in the realization that the crucified Jesus is the Christ. It is about the impact of that realization on the apostles, changing them from a dispirited, hopeless and weary group into zealous and confident fishers of men.

In short, the meaning of the story lies, as with the others, in its key phrases: *As day was breaking, there stood Jesus, and the disciples did not realize it. At the words, 'It is the Lord', Peter jumped in. And Jesus took bread and gave it to them. And Jesus said, 'Do you love me?' indicating the kind of death by which the disciple would glorify God. After this he said, 'Follow me.'*

The sacramental symbolism, I presume, is to be taken for granted in the reference to the bread, as it was in the story of the loaves and fishes. The story has told of the apostolic call, the universal mission, and the love which must characterize the Christian ministry. The Christian is to know that this is what he commits himself to when he receives bread from Christ's hands.

10. Explaining the Miracles Away?

It would be a useful exercise for the reader if he asked himself, at this point, what the explanation of the gospel miracle stories given above has done for him. Has it made the stories easier or more difficult, more intelligible or less? Has it enhanced these age-old stories for him, or destroyed them?

I imagine that for some the stories will have been permanently ruined. Before coming across this kind of explanation, they saw the miracles as unassailable evidence of the inbreaking of another world into our humdrum existence. Now the miracles seem to have been subtly explained away, and with them that other world, leaving only a sense of irretrievable loss.

Others may feel more sympathy for the approach taken above. They find it plausible enough and would have difficulty in arguing against it. But they too are finally left more than a little confused. Beforehand they at least knew, or thought they knew, the reality behind the miracle stories. Now they are no longer sure. They may be impressed by the dexterity with which I have justified my approach, but it leaves them rather disheartened. They may feel about it as the medieval theologian felt about the Athanasian Creed, when he called it the only statement about the Trinity which is strictly orthodox, but only at the cost of denying everything it says as soon as it says it!

It is for the sake of such readers that I want to make a final attempt to state the position as I see it.

JOHN THE THEOLOGIAN

The reason I have deliberately gone to the gospel of John to analyse the miracles is that he makes explicit the theology which I am convinced is present in the miracle stories of all four gospels. In the pages of Matthew, Mark and Luke we often fail to see it because it lies too deep beneath the surface. In John it is open and revealed. He has always been known as 'the theologian'. People think this makes his gospel more difficult to read than the other three. In fact it makes it easier: he has carefully spelled out the theological themes contained in the gospel stories for those not shrewd enough to work them out for themselves.

In trying to follow these theological themes, I have done my best to be honest. That is to say, I tried to avoid the temptation of reading into the stories what I wanted to find in them; I was anxious to follow only the clues John gave. If some of the clues are ambiguous and patient of more than one interpretation, there emerges from these stories nonetheless such a profound and wide-ranging theology that it has become impossible for me personally ever to read any miracle story again, even in Matthew, Mark or Luke, as if it were no more than a straight report of some remarkable event.

John is able to make explicit the theology contained in all the gospel miracle stories because he has turned our idea of metaphor on its head, and understands it in a way that is the very opposite of ours. For us, the piece of bread we had for breakfast is *real* bread, and Jesus can be called 'Bread' only metaphorically. John sees things the other way round. The true Bread is always the risen Christ: he is the ultimate reality. Anything else we may call 'bread' can only be a shadowy copy of him, and a metaphor. Or again, we call the father of a family the *real* father, and imagine that God can be called 'Father' only as a figure of speech. For John (and indeed for the author of Ephesians 3:15), God is the only real Father, and any other kind of fatherhood we know on earth is metaphorically named after him who was revealed to us in the death and resurrection of Jesus.

Throughout his gospel therefore, outside the miracle stories as well as in them, whether he is dealing with historical material or not, the one reality on which John's eyes are fixed is the crucified and risen Christ: everything else points to or is a 'sign' of that reality. John will even turn from a literal to a symbolic use of language and back again without pausing for

101

breath, because the sign or symbol, whether factual or verbal, is always being absorbed by the ultimate reality which it 'signposts' – the crucified Jesus who is the living Christ. That heavenly reality is the real Bread, the true Temple, the genuine Vine. And if everthing else is only a faint copy of it, then it matters little whether it be literal or symbolic, factual or verbal.

And yet, because the symbol is so closely united to the reality to which it points, we can never speak of a 'mere' symbol. It cannot be separated from the reality it signifies, which is Christ. I have not tried, in this book, to turn the miracle stories into 'mere' parables or illustrations or allegories of timeless truths. John does not think in those terms. None of the symbols he has used – wine, sight, life – are 'mere' words. They are always an embodiment of the eternal reality which is manifested in Jesus' death and resurrection.

SUSPENDING JUDGMENT

That is why I would wish to continue, to the very end, to suspend judgment about the historical or factual background of the miracle stories, about 'what really happened'. Firstly because we are no longer in a position to give a firm and clear answer to that question; I thought it more important to devote attention to the questions we can answer, on the theology contained in the stories. But then, also, because the answer to historical questions is only of secondary importance. And this is true not only of the miracle stories, but of any other page in the bible. No part of the bible offers us a blow by blow account of what occurred. Instead it offers us understanding, which is more important.

Some may ask whether it is legitimate to withhold judgment in this way, and whether it may not be sometimes essential to know what the actual historical reality was. Surely you have to decide, at least in certain cases, whether you are dealing with literal fact or not? How long can you remain impartial and neutral on this matter, without coming down on one side or the other?

The answer is that anyone who suspends judgment on this matter has already come down on one side. He has declared his hand by saying that all the miracle stories do not have to be 'miraculous' in the old sense. He has given judgment that it is possible to believe in Jesus and in the resurrection without the 'miraculous'.

> Faith is not believing that such things as the miraculous . . . really happened. It is believing in Jesus Christ as my Saviour, as the one in whom God has acted finally for my salvation. To such a faith, the historicity of this or that miracle in the gospel tradition is 'comparatively irrelevant'. (R. H. Fuller, *Interpreting the Miracles*, SCM, London, 1963, pp. 121–2).

The story of Cana as it now stands, for example, expresses the conviction of the first disciples that the coming of Christ was a life-giving wine, compared with which nothing that had gone before could warm the body or gladden the heart. Does it matter whether the event which lay behind this conviction was originally something that Jesus said rather than did? In either case the meaning remains the same, and depends for its validity on the disciples' experience of the resurrection. That was 'proof' enough, indeed the only proof possible, that in Jesus the Glory of God had walked among men. The text itself states this clearly enough in a phrase which John repeats again and again through the gospel:

> At the time his disciples did not understand this, but later, after Jesus had been glorified, they understood (John 2:22, see 12:16, 13:7, 14:26, 16:13, 20:9).

Ultimately the only question on the miracles that matters is, Where do we look for God? How do we expect him to show his hand? What kind of proof do we require to be certain that God is present in an event? When it came to the heart of the matter, the crux on Calvary, there were no more miracles in the old sense.

The preceding section may seem to suggest that there need not have been anything extraordinary at all about Jesus' life and ministry. That is not my conclusion. The tradition that Jesus was someone who performed marvels is so deeply rooted in the New Testament, and can be traced to such an early date, that most scholars conclude that the only explanation to account for this tradition is that marvels did occur. Eliminate all references to miracles in the gospel pages and there is no gospel left.

But the question posed in the opening chapters of this book remains: Does this prove anything? Most of the wonders attributed to Jesus are miracles of healing, and under this heading one could include his numerous cures of people who were 'possessed', many of whom would today be classified as suffering from nervous or psychiatric disorders. But these kinds of cures have been common throughout the history of religion, Christian and non-Christian alike, from the earliest days down to our own times. The pages of the New Testament itself bear witness to the fact that what Jesus did others were doing, or could do, and would even improve on (see the Jewish exorcists in Matthew 12:27; the disciples in Matthew 10:8, Mark 9:29, 16:17, Luke 10:19, John 14:12; rival preachers in Acts 19:13; Peter in Acts 3:7, 9:34; Paul in Acts 14:3, 19:12, 20:10, 2 Corinthians 12:12, etc.).

In other words, this kind of 'miracle' proves nothing except that a great deal of sickness, physical and mental, can be wondrously cured by methods of which we are, even now, scarcely aware. Some may wish to identify these as supernatural or preternatural, or even demonic. Most people today are more modest and confess that they are as yet unable to give a name to these powers; they seem to be part of the natural heritage of every man, even though in most cases they remain largely undeveloped.

To give these powers the generic title of 'faith-healing' adds little to our understanding of them, except to specify that they seem in general to depend on the trust and confidence of the patient or of the healer, usually of both. Some people may shrink from the word: it seems to them to downgrade the 'miracles' of Jesus, as if there is somehow something more suspect about a psychological explanation than about a frankly supernatural one. Yet the fact remains that more human sickness than we generally admit is psychosomatic in origin; it stems quite as much from an attitude of mind – habit, or resentment, or depression, or maladjustment – as on a purely functional or organic disorder. In cases of this kind, wonders have been worked, and continue to be worked, by the sheer will of the healer to free the patient from his bonds, and the confidence of the patient that the other has the power so to free him.

The evangelists bear witness that Jesus possessed this power to a remarkable degree. His whole life was evidence of his own wholeness and freedom. He showed matchless insight into the deeper and hidden source of man's sickness, and had utter confidence in the will of God to rescue men from the disintegrating forces that crippled their lives. Moreover, he was able to inspire others with the same confidence.

This is not to place cures of this kind outside the providence of God. It is only to try to pinpoint more accurately where God's providence is exercised, and how his activity is expressed and discerned.

DO MIRACLES HAPPEN TO ME?

But the problem does not end there. It is not only that others have done what Jesus did. The far deeper problem is that even if he had done things which no one else has ever done or could do, the modern reader of the gospel may still say, 'So what?' It must have been amazing grace for the lame and deaf and blind of 1900 years ago to be cured of their disabilities, but this hardly helps today's reader, especially if he is lame or deaf or blind. His handicap remains. In other words, however deep one's convictions that the stories of Jesus' miracles are historically reliable, that scarcely makes them 'good news'. Even Jesus' enemies were convinced that he was working wonders, and their reaction was to do away with him.

What makes the miracle stories 'gospel' is not their

historical accuracy but their *meaning*. Their meaning first of all for Jesus, who interpreted the cures that took place in response to his preaching as evidence that the Kingdom of God was breaking in on the world:

> If it is through the finger of God that I cast out devils, then know that the Kingdom of God has overtaken you (Luke 11:20).

He saw the healing of the sick who crowded round him as part of his mission to make God's world whole. He would have continued to see that as his mission, and to call for his disciples' commitment to it, even if no physical wonders had taken place.

But the miracle stories become 'gospel' for an even more important reason – because of the meaning given them by the evangelists, through whom alone we know of these wonders today. The evangelists told the miracle stories not simply to keep a record of certain extraordinary things which happened in the past, but to provide the believer with a test by which to gauge his own faith. The reader alone can tell, in his own experience, whether or not these stories are 'true'. Does Jesus still continue to work these wonders for him? If not, best keep the bible shut, as Sydney Carter advises:

> Your holy hearsay
> is not evidence;
> give me the good news
> in the present tense.
>
> What happened
> nineteen hundred years ago
> may not have happened –
> how am I to know?
>
> The living truth
> is what I long to see:
> I cannot lean upon
> what used to be.

106

So shut the Bible up
and show me how
the Christ you talk about
is living now.

The concern of this book has been that of the evangelist: to reveal the miracle stories as the good news in the present tense. They tell of Jesus the wonder worker. I know that they are true because I have experienced him doing the same wonders for me. I acknowledge him as my Lord not because in the days of his flesh he possessed more powerful magic than other wonder workers have done in their time. It is because he is risen from the dead, and therefore lives on as my contemporary, and continues to work similar wonders in me. It is my blindness he has lifted to allow me to see God through his eyes, my deafness he has taken away to let me hear the voice of God in a world I would be tempted to think of as closed to him. It is my leprosy he has cured by assuring me I am not an outcast but accepted by God, my paralysis he has healed by introducing me to a fullness of life I had not imagined possible. It is of my demonic possession he has freed me by revealing to me through his death and resurrection the devils that haunt me, my leaden feet he has enabled to walk – as he did – on elements which would otherwise engulf me.

Indeed, if these 'impossible' things had not happened to me, and did not continue to happen to me and to countless others day after day, I would see little point in reading of such things happening in the pages of the gospel.

Did the 'impossible' really take place? The answer is that the central claim of the Christian gospel is itself 'impossible' – that the Word of God became flesh and dwelt among us, that God was in Christ reconciling the world to himself. If anyone believes in that central 'impossibility', then it is rather pointless to keep asking questions about the historical accuracy of the miracle stories. It is rather as if the woman taken in adultery, having been sent away pardoned, could only remark on the fact that Jesus was wearing sandals at the time.

Some may express concern that the traditional teaching of the Church on miracles is being chiselled away by what has been said above. They may be afraid that this kind of scepticism on the subject of miracles, reverent though it be, is incompatible with statements to which the Christian community has committed itself over the centuries, namely that miracles *do* happen, that they *can* be known with certainty, and that they *prove* something about the divine origin of Christianity.

And yet statements to which the Church has committed itself across the years should never be considered in the abstract. No formulation of our faith, however solemn, can ever be an absolute. Only God can be that. Obviously the formulas in which the community has tried to encapsulate its experience of God express something that is deeply true, and it will always be the duty of subsequent generations to relive that experience of their fathers in the faith by means of those formulas. But it will also be the duty of later generations to ask why their forebears expressed themselves in the way they did. Because the truth is always greater than our formulations. We must not imagine that any age can capture it once for all and so absolve future generations from the need to join in the ongoing search.

It is interesting that solemn statements about miracles do not begin to make an appearance in Church documents until the late nineteenth century, the age of the rise of rationalism. The rationalist is the person who denies the possibility of the transcendent. For him, reality is a closed system, working on fixed laws which can be clearly defined, totally explained and fully understood. There is no reality other than that which can be seen, heard, touched or reasoned to. There is no future for the world other than that which is determined by the system itself.

Such a world has no room for mystery or for wonder, for the new or the unexpected. It is totally explicable in terms of observation and reasoning. Such a world needs no creator: it just happened. Less still does it need a saviour: it is either unsavable or it has to save itself.

Now there is always a danger, in combating someone else's opinion, of unconsciously adopting the opponent's viewpoint. The Church of the nineteenth century found itself in this position. In marshalling their arguments against rationalism, Christian theologians of the time found themselves unwittingly using rationalistic language. Instead of rejecting the rationalist closed-world view as an inadequate picture of reality, they themselves accepted it and then tried to prove that such a world nonetheless remained open, if only ever so slightly, to the transcendent.

But in such a world-view, the transcendent God can only be an outsider to the world. He has to be objectified into a superperson beyond the system, who must 'intervene' from outside and 'violate' the natural order from time to time to reveal that he exists. These interventions, the theologians claimed, are precisely the miracles of creation, of the incarnation, of the ministry of Jesus, and of the resurrection. Without them, we would have no means of knowing what God's will is, nor indeed would the majority of men know whether he exists at all.[1]

[1] The solemn statements made by the Roman Catholic Church on this subject reveal the world-view adopted by those who formulated them, and their apologetic concern. In 1840 the Strasbourg professor Louis *Bautain* was required to sign a statement that Jesus' miracles prove the truth of the Christian revelation, and that this proof remains valid today. In 1864 Pius IX listed as one of the errors to be included in his *Syllabus* the view that the miracles contained in the bible are only poetry. In 1870 the first *Vatican Council* decreed that miracles are an absolutely certain sign of God's revelation, adapted to the minds of all men, and it anathematized anyone who would say nay. In 1910 Pius X required of his professors a solemn *Antimodernist Oath* repudiating the view that miracles are not a proof of the divine origin of the Christian religion, or are not accommodated to the minds of men of 1910. In 1950 Pius XII, concerned about the persistence of 'modernist' views within the Church, issued the encyclical *Humani Generis* to insist (among other things) that the basic facts on which the Christian faith rests have been irrefutably established by proofs divinely granted us. It is interesting that, in 1964, the only reference to Jesus' miracles in the second *Vatican Council* speaks of them far more modestly – and biblically – as a sign of the fact that the Kingdom of God has arrived on earth (*Lumen Gentium*, 5).

But such a view of reality is not the only possible one. Indeed it is utterly alien to many thinking people today, for whom God is not an outsider to the whole process, but the supreme Insider, the mystery lying at the heart of all things, revealing himself above all in the lives of people. In such a view, the world is already open to the marvellous and the surprising, especially where people are concerned. There is no need to think in terms of some superperson who intervenes from without. Certainly the bible supposes no such superperson. In its view of reality, the whole world, extraordinary or ordinary, is an expression of the mystery that is God, and every rose that blooms is a 'miracle' capable of arousing thoughts that lie too deep for tears. Can an intervention that is as all-pervasive as that any longer be called 'intervention'?

The Church documents, in their time-bound language, have done no more than emphasize what the Judaeo-Christian tradition has always proclaimed – the redemptive presence of God in our world, especially in the lives of people. When this conviction is expressed in terms of a God who is added to his world, and separable from it, then 'intervention' is the only model in which that presence can be spoken of, and miracles must be regarded as interventions of that kind. But if God is already redemptively involved in man's becoming, if he is already graciously present to all human history, if the unexpected and the gratuitous and the marvellous are already woven into the fabric of our world, then we can no longer think of miracles in that way. What people call 'miracles' are simply the disclosure of a dimension of human life which would otherwise have remained hidden. And in that case the reality that underlies the miracle stories of the gospels has to be expressed in different terms. This book has tried to do that.

Nature . . . is not a closed definable system. The new takes place again and again . . . The ordinary events of life are not simply due to the unfolding of fixed laws . . . (but) the result of God's redemptive presence in human life and hence as much surprising and gratuitous as are miracles . . . Miracles are startling events that go against man's immediate expectations, but they are signs to men only if they call to

mind the ever startling grace of God operative in their lives
. . . To people who do not believe, miracles mean nothing
. . . Miracles are not violations of the natural order, helping
us to prove the existence of a transcendent God and the
loving concern he has for human life. Miracles are not even
divine signs revealing the power of God and confirming the
message preached in his name. Miracles . . . are simply
startling events that bring out the startling character
implicit in all of human life and hence have meaning only for
men who already acknowledge the marvellous as a dimension of human history (Gregory Baum, *Man Becoming*,
Seabury Press, New York, 1971, pp. 267–9).

WHAT IS SUPERNATURAL?

What has been said above may sound like an attempt to have
one's cake and eat it, to keep the gospel miracles without
needing to regard them as truly miraculous or supernatural.

The answer to this objection, of course, depends on where
one looks for the truly supernatural. There have been
agnostics throughout the ages whom the gospel miracles,
taken literally, have only managed to repel. This has surprised
Christian apologists, who thought that the gospel miracles
were tailor-made for the doubts of the agnostic: they would
stun him into belief. Instead, they have only put him off
Christianity, not attracted him to it. For him, this kind of
'supernatural' has nothing to say, and a Christianity which is
apparently based on it is something he cannot begin to take
seriously.

But it is not only agnostics who feel that way about the
gospel miracles. There are Christians too, and their number is
growing, who find the miracle stories as normally presented an
embarrassment rather than a joy, an obstacle to their faith not a
help. They feel that a Christ who could literally work prodigies
at will is no longer their brother, and would honestly prefer a
Christ who had less of an unfair advantage over them. They
would feel more at home with a Christ who was less of a

111

Captain Marvel and more like themselves, labouring under the human limitations in which they have to live their lives.

Nor is this a 'surrender to materialism and humanism', a capitulation to the 'spirit of the age'. Such Christians continue to search wholeheartedly for the truly supernatural, but they look for it, as scripture does, in the depths of nature itself rather than in violations of nature. They feel that the miracle stories, as they have been presented in the past, suppose an image of God which is unworthy of God, rather like the one at which the cartoonist Calman gently poked fun when he represented him on a cloud, wearing a worried frown, and saying, 'I think I left a volcano on somewhere.' The God whom Jesus preached is not the God who looks after things we cannot ourselves control, the absentee despot who occasionally intervenes to do superhuman things to inspire a salutary respect for him. He is the mystery of patient and suffering love present at the heart of all things, especially in the hearts of men. He does not show himself by force but by the manifest truth of his revelation. The truly supernatural is revealed not in works of shattering power, but in the quality of life he calls forth.

It has been the purpose of this book to show that Jesus' miracles reveal to us the face of this God. It is perhaps those who insist on a too literalistic interpretation of his miracles who are today hiding what he came to reveal. To demand that God should be an intervening God, who must present his credentials before he can be accepted, is to reduce God to an observable phenomenon. This surely is the worst kind of materialism, guaranteed to drive many thinking believers into apostasy.

Jesus worked miracles, but since he was a man they were the kind of miracles men can work. And so he presumed, quite naturally, that his disciples would work miracles greater than his own:

I tell you most solemnly,
whoever believes in me
will perform the same works as I do myself,
he will perform even greater works (John 14:12).

112

After all, would they not, under the inspiration of the Spirit he breathed out in his death on the cross, be able to feed the hungry and expel the demons that haunt mankind, to heal the sick and offer new life to men, in far greater numbers than he could ever hope to help in his own mortal lifetime? I do not see this as 'explaining the miracles away'. I see it as an invitation to understand them more deeply by accepting a frightening responsibility: I am called to work miracles myself.

11. Postscript

Since this book has tried to provide not only an outline of the gospel miracle stories, but also an introduction to the theology of John, I thought it would be useful to include the text of some radio talks I was asked to give on the opening chapters of John's gospel. They express, as simply as I can manage, the substance of what I have said here about John's theology. Fortunately John is a theologian who expresses all he has to say in each chapter, so that we miss nothing – except an opportunity for deeper reflection – by restricting ourselves to his opening pages.

The talks were preceded by a reading of John's text and a summarizing 'thought' for the day.

GOD'S WORD IS LOVE

Love someone, and you'll know God.

In the beginning was the Word:
and the Word was with God
and the Word was God.
He was with God in the beginning.
Through him all things came to be,
not one thing had its being but through him.
All that came to be had life in him
and that life was the light of men,
a light that shines in the dark,
a light that darkness could not overpower . . .
The Word was the true light
that enlightens all men;
and he was coming into the world.
He was in the world

that had its being through him,
and the world did not known him.
He came to his own domain
and his own people did not accept him.
But to all who did accept him
he gave power to become children of God (John 1 : 1–12).

There's a sense in which, when we speak of God, we really don't know what we're talking about. Because God wouldn't be God if he wasn't the ultimate Mystery, the Beyond, the reality that is always eluding our grasp.

So that if you and I are to have any contact with God at all, it's God who has to make the first move. We can't track him down by our own efforts. If we are to know God at all, he has to speak. What God speaks is his Word.

John begins his gospel with the magnificent statement that this Word was spoken by God from the very beginning. There is no time when God has not given himself away. He is like light, which betrays itself wherever it is. If you strike a match anywhere in the dark, it's dark no longer.

So there is no time and no place where those who are sensitive haven't been able to meet God, to hear God, to see God, in all kinds of ways. From the very beginning, the light came into the world to enlighten every man.

We who are sometimes tempted to think that we have a corner in God should be aware of this. Our faith is not meant to divide us from the rest of men, but to join us to them. We may boast of being sons of the Abraham who heard God's voice and responded so faithfully. But God can raise sons of Abraham from the stones, even from moon rocks; and each one of them is a witness to the fact that God has spoken his Word at all times, and in all places.

What God's word spells out is love. Yes, let's make all the necessary qualifications. Let's insist that we're talking about real love and not any imitation, that we're talking about a costly love and not a cheap one. But in the last analysis, the Word that gives God away, the Word that tells us what ultimately God is, is not authority, or power, or domination, but love.

115

And anyone who has ever heard that, however faintly, has heard the voice of God. And anyone who has ever responded, however imperfectly, has shown whose Father he's a child of.

Have you ever loved anyone, or been loved? You've heard God's Word. You have known God, and God has known you, even if you don't use his name. To all who have heard the Word of God he has given the power to become children of God.

LIFE ABUNDANT

In Jesus, God spoke so clearly, we call him the Word of God made flesh.

On the third day there was a wedding at Cana in Galilee. The mother of Jesus was there, and Jesus and his disciples had also been invited. When they ran out of wine, since the wine provided for the wedding was all finished, the mother of Jesus said to him, 'They have no wine.' Jesus said, 'Woman, why turn to me? My hour has not come yet.' His mother said to the servants, 'Do whatever he tells you.' There were six stone water jars standing there, meant for the ablutions that are customary among the Jews: each could hold twenty or thirty gallons. Jesus said to the servants, 'Fill the jars with water', and they filled them to the brim. 'Draw some out now' he told them 'and take it to the steward'. They did this; the steward tasted the water, and it had turned into wine. Having no idea where it came from – only the servants who had drawn the water knew – the steward called the bridegroom and said, 'People generally serve the best wine first, and keep the cheaper sort till the guests have had plenty to drink; but you have kept the best wine till now.' This was the first of the signs given by Jesus: it was given at Cana in Galilee. He let his glory be seen, and his disciples believed in him (John 2:1–11).

Six jars holding twenty gallons each makes 120 gallons. That's a lot of wine. That must have been some party!

There's a puritan streak in most of us which makes us a little uneasy with this story. We're frightened by the abuse we know we're all capable of. But there are people – and the people of the bible are among them – who take a more optimistic attitude towards God's gifts, and who know that wine was made to rejoice the hearts of men, and that there are occasions when rejoicing is not only in order, but positively necessary, like weddings.

And when people like that spoke about Kingdom Come, the day when all men's dreams would come true, and the hidden God men yearn to see would be revealed, they compared it to a wedding feast where no one would go thirsty.

John says that day came when Jesus walked the earth. The best wine had been kept till then, and there was a superabundance of it.

I have said already that the Word of God is not restricted to a chosen few. When Jesus appeared, it wasn't the first time that God had spoken. But in Jesus he spoke so clearly and unmistakably, his way of life was so transparent to God, his life and death expressed what God is so adequately, that we can only call him the Word of God made flesh, the embodiment in a human life of all that God means to us.

And those who knew Jesus, and understood the meaning of his life and death, were filled with a fullness they'd never experienced before. He manifested to them the Glory, which is another name for God. And the experience intoxicated them.

So what this story says to me is that if I look for God merely in institutions or customs, like church-going or saying night and morning prayers, merely in things like that, then I'm likely to be disappointed. At the vital moment, when it comes to the crunch, that kind of thing is always going to run out, like the wine at the wedding feast.

If you really want life abundant, says John, the kind that won't give out, then you've got to live in the Spirit of this man, who can turn water into wine, and hell into heaven. Believe me, says John, I've seen it. Why not try it yourself?

117

Whenever we're grateful, we glimpse the Kingdom of God.

There was one of the Pharisees called Nicodemus, a leading Jew, who came to Jesus by night and said, 'Rabbi, we know that you are a teacher who comes from God; for no one could perform the signs that you do unless God were with him.' Jesus answered:

'I tell you most solemnly,
unless a man is born from above,
he cannot see the kingdom of God.'

Nicodemus said, 'How can a grown man be born? Can he go back into his mother's womb and be born again?' Jesus replied:

'I tell you most solemnly,
unless a man is born through water and the Spirit,
he cannot enter the kingdom of God:
what is born of the flesh is flesh;
what is born of the Spirit is spirit:
Do not be surprised when I say:
You must be born from above.
The wind blows where it pleases;
you hear its sound,
but you cannot tell where it comes from
or where it is going.
That is how it is with all who are born of the Spirit'
(John 3:1–8).

Perhaps this reading makes you smile, the thought of a grown man going back into his mother's womb. For us, returning to the womb is an image of immaturity and insecurity. But for John the idea is simply a kind of deliberate mistake. His gospel is full of people who keep missing the point, so as to allow him to make the point more clearly, a second time.

The point he wants to make in this story of Nicodemus is that the kind of life Jesus calls people to is not – as we're always mistakenly imagining – a prize awarded to us for effort. It's a sheer gift, like our own birth, to which we contributed nothing. Only this birth comes from above, from God.

God alone can make us his children, by pouring on us his Spirit. We can't graduate to that title. What is born of the flesh can never be anything more than flesh, frail and perishable, here today and gone tomorrow. To have the kind of life that is rooted in God we have to be born of the Spirit.

What Spirit is John talking of? The Spirit of Jesus. And how do we receive that? By standing, as it were, under the cross of Jesus. That, John says, is where Jesus breathed out the Spirit. That, John says, is where water poured out of his open side, the water which was to irrigate a parched world. Unless a man is born of that water and that Spirit, he cannot enter the Kingdom of God. Unless a man is willing to be inspired by, to be invaded by the kind of Spirit with which Jesus breathed his last, he'll never become what Gods calls him to be.

And who could be described in those terms? Only a few people? That would be strange! Surely there's an enormous number of people who have lived in the Spirit that characterized the death of Jesus, a Spirit of courage and selflessness, a Spirit of forgiveness and reconciliation, a Spirit of love and compassion, a Spirit of impatience with all that enslaves and degrades and corrupts, but of infinite patience with people.

The Spirit certainly blows where it pleases, calling all men to fullness and freedom. And when they respond to that call, they are born of the Spirit, whether they know it or not.

The question is, Do they recognize this as a gift from above? We want so much to feel that we've earned what we've got, that we're paying our own way. And yet if we've ever deeply reflected on the love with which we are loved, we know we could never earn that, it's sheer gift. And even more so the power of loving that lies in our own hearts. To be grateful for that, even without knowing whom to thank, is to be born of the Spirit and to enter the Kingdom of God.

Life is always stronger than death, and love has a power that evil cannot match.

Jesus came to the Samaritan town called Sychar, near the land that Jacob gave to his son Joseph. Joseph's well is there and Jesus, tired by the journey, sat straight down by the well. It was about the sixth hour. When a Samaritan woman came to draw water, Jesus said to her, 'Give me a drink.' His disciples had gone into the town to buy food. The Samaritan woman said to him, 'What? You are a Jew and you ask me, a Samaritan, for a drink?' – Jews, in fact, do not associate with Samaritans. Jesus replied:

'If you only knew what God is offering
and who it is that is saying to you:
"Give me a drink",
you would have been the one to ask,
and he would have given you living water.'

'You have no bucket, sir,' she answered 'and the well is deep: how could you get this living water? Are you a greater man than our father Jacob who gave us this well and drank from it himself with his sons and his cattle?' Jesus replied:

'Whoever drinks this water
will get thirsty again;
but anyone who drinks the water that I shall give
will never be thirsty again:
the water that I shall give
will turn into a spring inside him,
welling up to eternal life' (John 4:5–14).

I have already said that, for John, the theme of water always reminds him of what happened on Calvary. It was at a time when Jesus was wearied, exhausted and desperate with thirst that he himself offered to men the water which could quench their thirst for ever. The parched man became a fountain of living water.

We're talking again about the Spirit of Christ, or the Holy Ghost as we've come to call him in our quaint English. Many people still think of the Spirit as a kind of ghostly third person who, they are told, is of vital importance to their spiritual lives, but they can't quite see why. Perhaps it would help if we realized that the Holy Spirit is nothing other than that Spirit of love in which Jesus lived his whole life, and which he yearned to share with all men.

And this he did, says John, when he died. Because it was only in his death that Jesus, whose whole life had spoken of God, became the Word of God so clearly that no one could any longer be mistaken about what God is like. God is like this figure on the cross; he totally accepts and suffers the worst that men can do, and still forgives.

So in death, Jesus, the Man who is for others, reveals that God is like that from all eternity, totally for others, totally on our side against the forces which would destroy us. Indeed it is only because of that, that the forces of evil are neutralized and transformed. Because life is always stronger than death, and love has a power that evil cannot match.

It's in this Spirit that Jesus lived his whole life. His death meant that, instead of sharing that Spirit with only the few who spoke to him and heard him, he was now free of all limitations, and could pour out that Spirit on all who understood the meaning of his death. And those who drank of that Spirit said that they would never thirst for anything else. It had become like a living fountain of water in their own hearts, this secret of living in God's own way. To share the Spirit of Christ, to live in the way he lived and died, is to know God as he did.

I find it interesting that John puts all these reflections in the setting of Samaria, that is right outside the circle of those who normally heard Jesus. Doesn't this imply that what Jesus said and did is not meant simply for a select in-group, but for everyone, for all listeners to 'Thought for the Day', whether they're religious or not. And if their lives are more effective in bringing about the reconciliation of all men than mine is, what does it mean to call myself a follower of Jesus?

FOLLOWING THE WAY OF CHRIST

Anybody who works for peace among men is already following the way of Christ.

The Samaritan woman said to Jesus, 'Our fathers worshipped on this mountain, while you say that Jerusalem is the place where one ought to worship.' Jesus said:

'Believe me, woman, the hour is coming
when you will worship the Father
neither on this mountain nor in Jerusalem.
You worship what you do not know;
we worship what we do know:
for salvation comes from the Jews.
But the hour will come –
in fact it is here already –
when true worshippers will worship the Father
in Spirit and truth:
that is the kind of worshipper the Father wants.
God is Spirit,
and those who worship
must worship in Spirit and truth.'

The woman said to him, 'I know that Messiah – that is Christ – is coming; and when he comes he will tell us everything.' 'I who am speaking to you,' said Jesus 'I am he' (John 4:20–6).

John is saying a lot more in this reading than that we should avoid sham and humbug and lip-service in religion. The word 'Spirit' in John's gospel always reminds us of what happened on Calvary. The Spirit in which God must be worshipped is the Spirit of the crucified Christ.

122

They were having a very heated argument, in New Testament times, about which was more pleasing to God, the temple which the Samaritans had built on the mountain overlooking the well where Jesus was sitting, or the temple which the Jews had built on the hill of Jerusalem. People still argue in that way; only the place names have changed.

John is saying that the argument is rather pointless. They may both be pleasing to God, or both unpleasing. What is certain is that God isn't someone you can meet in a building. But you can meet him in the Body of Christ. That is the Temple from which, as the poetry of the Old Testament had put it, a stream would pour out to bring new life to a thirsty world.

The Body of Christ. We're always tempted to try to find our relationship with God outside of institutions, and to make it rather abstract and ethereal. But the Body of Christ is always bodily. His risen Body is made up of those who live by his Spirit of self-sacrifice and forgiveness and love. There's a famous Peanuts cartoon in which Charlie Brown says, in a mood we all recognize, 'I love mankind: it's people I can't stand.' Well, however unpromising we may look, people are the only material there is for making up the Body of Christ, the true temple in which God is worshipped in Spirit and in truth.

I've said often enough that anybody who works for peace among men is already following the way of Christ. All I want to add here is that if I don't live my faith in the company of other people, who share Christ's Spirit with me, how do I know that it is the Spirit of Christ?

So today's thought forms a sequence with the rest. On Monday we thought of God speaking his Word, and giving himself away to all men, at all times, in the love they have experienced. On Tuesday we listened to a disciple who said that love was most eloquently spoken in the life of someone who turned the water of his life into wine. On Wednesday we thought of that love, which everyone has experienced, however anonymously, as being a gift from above. On Thursday we thought of that love as breathed out by the dying Jesus. And today's thought is that no one can live that love on his own. The Body of Christ can't be discovered except in people.

The reading ends with the words, 'The hour will come – in fact it is here already'; 'The Messiah is coming – in fact he is speaking to you.' John uses the phrase frequently as a warning. We keep imagining that Kingdom Come is impossible here and now. There was a Kingdom Come in bible times, and there will be a Kingdom Come in the remote future. But it's not possible now, not in the mess our lives and our world is in.

John says, 'But it is. The reality I've been talking about is here and now. Why don't you grasp it? It's in your hands.'

A Plan of John's Gospel

There have been many attempts to discover what plan John or his editors had in mind when drawing up the fourth gospel. I include this page to let the reader see at a glance the plan I have followed. I have asterisked the passages on which I have offered some commentary, and double-asterisked the eight miracles stories in the text.

1. *Table of Contents:* Jesus is the Life, Light
   and Glory of God   1:1–18★
   Witnesses confirm this (Jordan)   1:19–51
   Signs illustrate this (Cana, Temple)   2:1–25★★

2. *Jesus the Life of God*
   The New Life of the Spirit (Nicodemus)   3:1–36★
   Worship in the Spirit (Samaritan woman)   4:1–42★
   Life to the dying (The dying boy)   4:43–54★★
   Life to the dying (The cripple)   5:1–18★★
   The Discourse on the source of life   5:19–47
   The Bread of Life   6:1–15★★
   Victory over the grave   6:16–21★★
   The Discourse on the Bread of Life   6:22–71★
   Tabernacles: the Water of Life (Nicodemus)   7:1–53★

3. *Jesus the Light of God*
   The Light of the world versus darkness   8:12–59★
   Enlightenment of the blind man   9:1–41★★
   Blind shepherds and the good Shepherd
   (Jordan)   10:1–42★

4. *The Life and Light show forth God's Glory*
   (Lazarus)   11:1–57★★

5. *Jesus the Glory of God*
   Preliminaries to the Passion   12:1–50

The glory of the Servant   13:1–32
Jesus' departure is his coming in the
    Spirit   13:33–14:31
Love is the fruit of the Vine   15:1–16:4
Jesus' departure is his coming in the
    Spirit   16:4–33
To love is to share in the glory   17:1–26
The glory of Jesus' passion and death   18:1–19:42
The glory of Jesus' resurrection   20:1–31

6. *Appendix:* Peter shares in the glory   21:1–25**